Our Shared Japan

First published in 2007 by
The Dedalus Press
13 Moyclare Road
Baldoyle
Dublin 13
Ireland
www.dedaluspress.com

Editor: Pat Boran

This selection copyright © The Dedalus Press, 2007
Introduction copyright © Irene De Angelis & Joseph Woods, 2007
The acknowledgements on pages 230—232 constitute
an extension of this copyright notice.

All rights reserved.
No part of this publication may be reproduced in any form or by
any means without the prior permission of the publisher.

ISBN 978 1 904556 81 7 (bound)
ISBN 978 1904556 82 4 (paper)

Dedalus Press titles are represented in North America
by Syracuse University Press, Inc., 621 Skytop Road,
Suite 110, Syracuse, New York 13244, and in the UK by
Central Books, 99 Wallis Road, London E9 5LN.

Typesetting and Design: Pat Boran & Beth Romano.
Printed and bound by ColourBooks,
Unit 105 Baldoyle Industrial Estate, Dublin 13, Ireland.

Cover image: *Coloured Signs 'd'*
Etching, 36 x 36 cm (20 x 20 cm image)
copyright © Felim Egan (www.felimegan.ie)

Sponsored by the Cultural Division of the Department of Foreign Affairs

The Dedalus Press receives financial
assistance from An Chomhairle Ealaíon
/ The Arts Council, Ireland

Our Shared Japan

An Anthology of Contemporary Irish Poetry

❧

Edited, with an Introduction, by
Irene De Angelis and Joseph Woods

Afterword by
Seamus Heaney

THANKS

For help, advice and assistance of various kinds, the editors wish to express their sincere gratitude to the following:

Donatella Abbate Badin, David Burleigh, Melita Cataldi, Felim Egan, David Ewick, Seamus Heaney, Catherine Leydon, Peter McMillan, Ciaran Murray, Dennis O'Driscoll, Chie Oda, Mitsuko Ohno, Masazumi Toraiwa; the staff of Poetry Ireland: Jane O'Hanlon, Anna Boner, Moira Cardiff, Deryn O'Brien, Paul Lenehan, David Maybury and our two Poetry Ireland interns, Alan Murrin and Jessica Morton, who worked very hard on the typescript; Dedalus Press intern Beth Romano for all of assistance on and dedication to the project; Francis X. O'Donoghue from the Cultural Division of the Department of Foreign Affairs who was so helpful and took such a keen interest in the book; and, finally, our thanks are due to Dedalus Press Editor Pat Boran who, throughout the project, and despite the complexities of steering the anthology to completion in the limited time period available, managed to do so with grace and patience.

Contents

INTRODUCTION / xv

❧

FERGUS ALLEN
Battue / 3

DERMOT BOLGER
First Japanese Sonnet / 4
Second Japanese Sonnet / 4
Westport Tanka / 5

PAT BORAN
A Natural History of Armed Conflict / 6
Way of Peace / 6

DAVID BURLEIGH
Haiku / 8

PADDY BUSHE
Frog Song / 9
Lótus Bhéarra / Lotus in Beara / 9

RUTH CARR
In Hokkaido / 12
Mushroom / 12

CIARAN CARSON
The Rising Sun / 14
Green Tea / 14
The Irish Exile Michael Hinds / 15
The Blue Shamrock / 16

Fuji Film / 16
Banana Tree / 17
February Fourteen / 18
from *Belfast Confetti: Haiku versions* / 18

DEIRDRE CARTMILL
Karaoke in the Glasshouse / 21

JUANITA CASEY
Zen and Now / 23

AUSTIN CLARKE
Japanese Print / 25

PATRICK COTTER
A Richard Brautigan Moment / 26

YVONNE CULLEN
Kabuki / 27

TONY CURTIS
Siren Off Inisheer / 29
Northern Haiku / 29
Seven Haiku for Sahoko's Drawing / 30

GERALD DAWE
The Moon Viewing Room / 32

PATRICK DEELEY
Bashō on the Dodder / 34

GREG DELANTY
The Speakeasy Oath / 36

MOYRA DONALDSON
Kobi / 38
Bamboo / 38
Carp / 38

KATIE DONOVAN
Blossom Time / 39

MARY DORCEY
Grace / 41

KATHERINE DUFFY
Nightingales of the Little Emperors / 42

SEÁN DUNNE
The Frail Sprig / 43
The Art of Tea / 44
A Shrine for Lafcadio Hearn, 1850-1904 / 46
Shiatsu Sequence / 47

PAUL DURCAN
Wild Sports of Japan / 50
6.30 a.m., 13 January 2004, Hokkaido Prefecture / 50
Raftery in Tokyo / 50
The Journey Home from Japan / 51
Facing Extinction / 51

DESMOND EGAN
Hiroshima / 53

JOHN ENNIS
Watching the Descent of Yuichiro Miura / 54

PETER FALLON
World Peace / 56

GERARD FANNING
Week-end Away / 57

ANDREW FITZSIMONS
Worlds / 58
The Risen Tide / 58
The Autumn Night / 58
A Letter / 59

vii

Ornaments / 59
The Human / 59
Shunkashūto / 60

ANTHONY GLAVIN
from *'Living in Hiroshima'*
Ground Zero / 61
Magic! / 61
Aioi Bridge / 61
A Month Early / 62
Nostalgia / 62
The Domei News Agency / 62
Museum Time / 63

MARK GRANIER
The Great Wave / 64

PAMELA GREENE
Waiting for You / 65

EAMON GRENNAN
Sunshine, Salvation, Drying Shirt / 67

MAURICE HARMON
Japanese Garden / 69
Afternoon Tea / 70

MICHAEL HARTNETT
from *'Inchicore Haiku'* / 71

FRANCIS HARVEY
A Tanka and Four Haiku / 73

SEAMUS HEANEY
1.1.87 / 74
The Strand / 74
Fiddleheads / 74
Midnight Anvil / 75

RACHAEL HEGARTY
There is No Love in Hykyu / 77

JOHN HEWITT
Gloss, on the Difficulties of Translation / 78

JOHN HUGHES
Nagasaki / 79

PEARSE HUTCHINSON
Sneachta i gCuach Airgid / 80
Snow in a Silver Bowl / 81
Koan / 86

BIDDY JENKINSON
Tóraíocht Tai Haku *sna plandlannaí* / 87

FRED JOHNSTON
The Blue Whale / 89

EILEEN KATO
Sakurajima / 90

NEVILLE KEERY
Far Away / 91

THOMAS KINSELLA
Old Harry / 92

MATT KIRKHAM
Unfinished Haiku / 95

ANATOLY KUDRYAVITSKY
Unobana in Full Bloom / 96

MICHAEL LONGLEY
A Gift of Boxes / 98
A Grain of Rice / 99

A Pair of Shoes / 99
The Weather in Japan / 99
Birds & Flowers / 100
White Water / 101

BRIAN LYNCH
The Tea Ceremony / 102

DEREK MAHON
The Snow Party / 103
Bashō in Kinsale / 104

AIDAN CARL MATHEWS
Bashō's Rejected Jottings / 106

JOHN McAULIFFE
Japan / 112

JAMES McCABE
from *'Cliara Haiku I—XXX'* / 113

THOMAS McCARTHY
Japanese Bell / 115

MEDBH McGUCKIAN
The Flower Master / 116
The Butterfly Farm / 116
The Bird Calendar / 117

PETER McMILLAN
Broken Ink Landscape / 119
from Hyakunin Isshu / 122

TED McNULTY
Dreaming in Japanese / 123

PAULA MEEHAN
The First Day of Winter / 124

DOROTHY MOLLOY
Four Haikus / 125

SINÉAD MORRISSEY
Goldfish / 126
Night Drive in Four Metaphors / 127
Between Here and There / 128
Nagasawa in Training / 129
To Encourage the Study of Kanji / 130

PAUL MULDOON
The Narrow Road to the Deep North / 131
Sushi / 131
The Point / 133
Nightingales / 134
from *'Hopewell Haiku' / 135*

GERRY MURPHY
The Ferbane Haiku / 140
Haiku for Norman McCaig / 140
Ballynoe Haiku / 141

NUALA NÍ DHOMHNAILL
Sneachta / Snow / 142

JULIE O'CALLAGHAN
Time / 143
Lady Hyobu / 143
A View of Mount Fuji / 144
Two Lines / 145
21st Century Pillow Book / 146
Calligraphy / 150

JOHN O'DONNELL
The Wave / 152

MARY O'DONNELL
10 Haikus on Love and Death / 153

DESMOND O'GRADY
from *'Summer Harvest Renga'* / 155

TOM O'MALLEY
from *'Seasonal Haiku'* / 157

CAITRÍONA O'REILLY
Netsuke / 159

FRANK ORMSBY
Six Haiku / 161

CATHAL Ó SEARCAIGH
Duine Corr / Odd Man Out / 162
Pilleadh an Deoraí / Exile's Return / 165

MICHEAL O'SIADHAIL
Tsunami / 166

EOGHAN Ó TUAIRISC
Three sections from 'Aifreann na Marbh'
1. Introitus / Introit / 168
2. Kyrie / Kyrie / 170
3. Graduale / Gradual / 176

JUSTIN QUINN
On Speed / 178

PADRAIG ROONEY
In the Bonsai Garden / 180
Sukiaki / 181
The Night Golfer / 182

MARK ROPER
from *Whereabouts* / 183

GABRIEL ROSENSTOCK
A Handful of Haiku in Irish and English / 184
Farrera / 186

RICHARD RYAN
Five Senryū / 194

JOHN W. SEXTON
Issa in the golden corridor / 195

EILEEN SHEEHAN
claiming it / 197

JAMES SIMMONS
Empire / 198

PETER SIRR
In the Japanese Garden / 199

GERARD SMYTH
December Moon / 201

BILL TINLEY
Jeanne Hébuterne / 202

JOSEPH WOODS
Sailing to Hokkaido / 204
Where the Word for Beautiful is Clean / 205
New Year's Day, Nagasaki / 206
Triptych / 207
Persimmon / 208

MACDARA WOODS
Rosbeg, July 2nd, 1970 / 209

AFTERWORD
SEAMUS HEANEY: *Petals on a Bough* / 211

ABOUT THE EDITORS / *219*

NOTES ON CONTRIBUTORS / *219*

ACKNOWLEDGEMENTS / *230*

Introduction

❧

Almost ten years after the publication of Pierre Loti's *Madame Chrysanthème* (1887), the Greek-Irish scholar Lafcadio Hearn was granted Japanese citizenship (1896) and changed his name to Yakumo Koizumi. Two decades later, W.B. Yeats's imagination seems haunted by Japanese Noh drama, as he had known it through Ernest Fenollosa and Ezra Pound.

In compiling an anthology of Irish poetry about Japan, one cannot but be aware of, even perhaps haunted by, both Yeats's engagement with Japanese culture and Hearn's earlier engagement and actual encounter. Though both writers are present in the poems gathered here, both explicitly and implicitly, the poems in this anthology represent responses to the subject and influence of Japan as it has developed over the past half century, a period which coincides—though hardly accidentally—with the opening of diplomatic relations between the two countries in 1957.

An increased interest in Japanese culture is certainly evident in the works of Irish poets from this time, and may have been driven by a worldwide interest in Japan in this period, its economic rise and increased profile among other nations. Even so, and as is so often the case, it was surely fed and nourished by timely publications such as *The Penguin Book of Japanese Verse*, (Geoffrey Bownas and Anthony Thwaite, 1964) and volumes such as Matsuo Bashō's, *The Narrow Road to the Deep North and Other Travel Sketches* which appeared in English translation in 1966. These books had the impact of introducing Japanese poetry to a wider readership. There were other titles too (mostly American editions), to which one might add the translations of Arthur Waley and Kenneth Yasuda, and perhaps no less crucially, the poems of American poets such as Cid Corman and Gary Snyder.

The appearance in 1973 of Derek Mahon's masterly and now iconic poem 'A Snow Party' seemed to mark a decisive point. From the mid-1970s on, Japanese subjects appear with some frequency in Irish poems, and forms like the haiku are adopted and, increasingly, adapted to an Irish medium. (One might reasonably argue that, as in the case of the sonnet and its Italian origins, the haiku has long since become an international form which looks back to, but is not bound by its roots in Japanese composition.)

Considering the geographical distance which separates Ireland and Japan, with both countries occupying opposite ends of Eurasia, it seems by any criteria extraordinary the interest contemporary Irish poets take in Japan. In focusing on their work, we have not set out to neglect or overlook a tradition, but rather to leave 'room to rhyme' for a plurality of new voices that stand in a line of continuity with the past. Moreover, on the occasion of the 50th anniversary of diplomatic relations between Ireland and Japan, it seemed particularly appropriate that this publication should include writings in English and in Irish from the early 1960s, as well as more recent work which also reflects elements of the changing nature, and composition, of Ireland itself.

The word anthology literally means 'collection of flowers', and these poems are, to paraphrase Paddy Bushe, 'floral strangers' on this occasion travelling from West to East. They share what Seamus Heaney has called the 'Japanese effect', a definition which he first used in his 2000 Lafcadio Hearn Lecture. It is a great privilege and an honour to include here the abridged version of that same unpublished essay, which he kindly prepared for this volume.

A full understanding of the meaning and interplay of the poems selected would require a complex analysis necessarily limited here to a few considerations. Generally speaking, on a stylistic level some Irish poets have found the 'true note' and the 'clean line' of Japanese haiku refreshing. Harold G. Henderson's 1958 *Introduction to Haiku* and the aforementioned *Penguin Book of Japanese Verse* (1964) have been, at least for some of them, two 'little bibles'. The idea of 'writing by subtraction' has often led Irish poets, in different ways, to search for a new style. The Japanese 'newness' coincides, in most cases, with an effort to visually isolate the word on the page —the blank space is loaded with meaning. Interestingly, as early as 1913 the German scholar Kuno Meyer spoke of spareness as a central feature of the early Irish lyric. When Yeats speculated on the "Noble Plays of Japan", Meyer wrote:

> It is a characteristic of these poems that in none of them do we get an elaborate or sustained description of any scene or scenery, but rather a succession of pictures and images which the poet, like an impressionist, calls up before us by light and skilful touches. Like the Japanese, the Celts were always quick to take an artistic hint; they avoid the obvious and the commonplace; the half-said thing to them is dearest.
>
> (—*Ancient Irish Poetry*, 1913)

Irish poets whose writing displays a 'Japanese effect' do not necessarily experiment with haiku, tanka or other traditional Japanese forms. It is true that short Irish poetry is 'imagistic, aphoristic, [and] epigrammatic' (Ormsby 2000), and generally suggests a fuller picture by a few brush strokes. However, readers who expect this to be an anthology of short Irish poetry—or of Irish haiku—will be surprised by the range of poems that have been selected, including well-known pieces side-by side with less familiar work. The 'Japanese effect' in contemporary poetry does not only refer to style, but to the various unpredictable ways in which Japan has shaped the poets' imagination —in Ireland and the rest of the world. All of the contributors show a sincere interest in Japanese culture. Their poetry is not only informed by reading, but also by culture at a non-verbal level, particularly the visual arts, ink calligraphy and the crafts. In some cases, it was the direct contact with Japan which impressed their imaginations. In a broader context, Japan has created a new poetic wor-*l*-d, or, to appropriate a famous definition, it has shaped "Japan(s) of the mind".

The title of this anthology, *Our Shared Japan*, comes from the poem 'The Frail Sprig' by the late Seán Dunne:

> —a dream
> from our shared Japan and its snow
> over leaves afloat on streams.

Part prayer, part vision, it typifies what is best about the shared experience this anthology records and celebrates.

Irene De Angelis & Joseph Woods
August 2007

Our Shared Japan

FERGUS ALLEN

Battue

The origami-master folded away his smile
And swept his extended family into the litter-bin
To be eaten by paper tigers.

DERMOT BOLGER

First Japanese Sonnet

    Boots clatter the stile
But still create no echo
    Trees line the avenue
In pale light without shadow.
    As I enter the clearing
Beneath overhanging trees
    A familiar ghost appears

    Who stares as I rise,
And soar upwards in sleep
    Past the ruined house
In turbulent waves of heat,
    Calling out as I wake
Having almost once again
    Recognised his face.

Second Japanese Sonnet

    Through a tiny entrance
Hooves have churned to mud
    We enter the glistening forest,
Breathless with excited love.
    We stumble intuitively
Along a narrow glistening path
    To that forest clearing

Where the trees catch fire
And bright birds fly shrieking up
    As the spores burst open:
I never want to leave your warmth
    Even after I have come
And the gale recedes towards sleep
    And jaded birds fly down.

Westport Tanka

In this hotel room
Ribboned moonlight of your skin
Coming through half-drawn blinds.
I enter this new frontier
Where your love must guide me in.

PAT BORAN

A Natural History of Armed Conflict

The wood of the yew
made the bow. And the arrow.
And the grave-side shade.

Way of Peace

i.m. Eamon Keating

In Adidas runners
and white karate suit
with the simple crest—

a dove round a fist,
Wado Ryu,
the way of peace—

down the Downs,
past the gate house gate,
a chubby druid,

a breathing oak,
a shifting mountain,
following patterns

modelled on monkeys,
eagles and cranes,
stray dogs and dragons,

bird man of Portlaoise,
puff-jowled adder,
dancing bear,

a man in his 60s
somehow still
sane enough to play;

and me, 16,
hidden among trees,
glimpsing the way.

DAVID BURLEIGH

Haiku

Glittering spaceships
moving closer together
in the airless dark
      (Tanabata Festival)

Trapped inside a pot
at the bottom of the sea
the octopus dreams

Bootprints on the sand
and the whorls of ammonites
on ancient lava

The vanishing squid
leaves everything behind it
in a cloud of ink

The candlemaker dips
one hand in liquid wax—
a wild peony

PADDY BUSHE

Frog Song

Spring. In the flooded paddies
Rice stalks shoot fresh green
From their own reflections.

I walk along narrow ridges
Between paddies. Paths dip
Into sod walls and out again.

My stretched arms bank
Left and right, hold me
In exquisite balance.

The air is pulsing with frogs,
All of them on the one note:
Bashō… Bashō … Bashō…

Lótus Bhéarra

Is maith is cuimhin liom é,
An mhaidin aerach úd i mBéarra,
Spéir agus farraige fite fuaite
In aon ghealghoirme amháin,
Aiteann agus fraoch á mealladh isteach
I gcroithloinnir sin an chiúnais.
Is cuimhin liom an bóithrín casta

Go dtí an *Beara Dzogchen Retreat Centre*
A cheapfá a bheith díreach ar tí
Titim le faill, ach a dhein lúb obann
Aniar aduaidh ar féin agus timpeall
Ar linn sa bhfothain, niamhrach faoin ngréin.

Agus ansiúd ina lár, tá's ag Dia
Gan choinne ar domhan leis,
Bhí lótus corcra spréite romhainn,
Stróinséar blátha ón Domhan Toir,
Chomh cluthar sin go samhlófá é féin
Agus a sheacht shinnsear lótus roimhe
A bheith lonnaithe i lár na linne
Leis na cianta Béarracha.

Lótus sa linn,
Suíochán don Bhúda,
I measc fraoch agus aiteann Bhéarra,
An Búda sa linn, linn an Bhúda,
Dord na linne ag éirí ón lótus
Mar anál leoithneach,
Mar chumhracht oirthearach
In iarthar Bhéarra.
Sea is cuimhin liom an mhaidin
Aerach i mBéarra,
Is cuimhin liom an linn.

Lotus in Beara

It still breezes through my mind,
That airy morning in Beara,
The sea and the sky one

Seamless blue mantle,
Furze and heather seduced
Into that shimmering calm.

I remember the twisting boreen
To the Beara Dzogchen Retreat Centre,
That you'd think was about to
Topple over a cliff, but that turned
Back on itself out of the blue
Around a sheltered, sunlit pool.

And in the middle of the pool, God knows
Where on earth it blew in from,
A purple lotus spread itself under the sun,
A floral stranger from the East
Looking so snug that you'd imagine itself
And its seed, breed and generation
Had been settled in the pool
Since the time of the Flood.

A lotus in a pool,
A cushion for the Buddha
Among the heather and furze of Beara,
Buddha in the pool, the pool of Buddha,
The pool's prayer lilting through the lotus
In a breeze like a breath
Of eastern incense
On the western tip of Beara.

Yes, I remember that airy
Morning in Beara, and my mind still
Plunges deep in the pool.

RUTH CARR

In Hokkaido

In Hokkaido
the Japanese crane
in long black stockings and feather boa
picks her way through dancing snow
now you see her
now you don't.

Symbol of happiness
perched on stilts
like tentative thoughts of summer
she persists
where bears are baited in concrete pits
in Hokkaido.

Mushroom

I am rinsing milk white mushrooms
under the tap. Your mouth opens birdlike
to gulp all the world it can,

incautious and whole.
A sliver of white in all that pink—
the first tooth is through.

A girl's voice on the airwaves
shocked by the hole
where her sister's cheek should be,

she can see right through to the teeth.
Thousands of splinters mosaic her child form,
this is the nuclear act embedded in flesh.

When she dies, her mother begs
Bury me with her.
Please, bury me with her.

I am watching skin peel like paint
plants recoil into themselves
seeking their own shadow.

Dust blooms with each step
as this wave burns us up,
but not to ashes.

Fifty years on
a girl's voice on the airwaves
fragments everything.

On the blank white space that is a mushroom
I visualise a mushroom field at dawn.
I drop one and it's gone.

CIARAN CARSON

The Rising Sun

As I was driven into smoky Tokyo,
The yen declined again. It had been going down
All day against the buoyant Hibernian Pound.
Black rain descended like a harp arpeggio.

The Professor took me to a bonsai garden
To imbibe some thimblefuls of Japanese poteen.
We wandered through the forest of the books of Arden.
The number of their syllables was seventeen.

I met a maiden of Hiroshima who played
The hammer dulcimer like psychedelic rain.
The rising sun was hid behind a cloud of jade.

She sang to me of Fujiyama and of Zen,
Of yin and yang, and politics, and crack cocaine,
And Plato's caverns, which are measureless to men.

Green Tea

I saw a magnified red dot on a white field.
I saw the terraces and pyramids of salt.
I saw a towering mushroom cloud of cobalt.
I made sure my papers had been signed and sealed.

The writing everywhere on walls illegible to me.
The faces in the crowds unrecognisable.
The labyrinth to which I hadn't got the key.
Investing in the Zen is inadvisable.

Zeno made a gesture with his disembodied hand.
A landscape wafted into being from his brush.
The flow of water is represented by sand.

If anything, I think I drank too much green tea.
The snows of Fujiyama had all turned to slush.
Hibernia beckoned from across the blue sea.

The Irish Exile Michael Hinds

Your air mail had a border like the Tricolor.
I slit it open with a knife of Damask steel,
As it exuded perfumes of a humidor
Replete with odorous tobacco and smoked eel.

Included was a Russian doll, a crystal rock
Of salt, a miniature of Japanese poteen,
A pack of cigarettes called Peace, a single sock,
A plan of ancient Tokyo, a sprig of green.

I took it I'd to meet you in the Vodka Bar
Beneath the rising moon of Gorgonzola cheese,
From whence you'd drive me in your toy Toyota car

Through intersections where the stop and go are garbled,
Where fluent crowds converge in milling Japanese,
In sequences of poppy, amber, emerald.

The Blue Shamrock

Now they rehearse their ancient music on the harp,
And blow blue music from the bonsai bamboo flute,
The President is talking to the ancient carp
Which swims in green gloom in the Pisces Institute.

Like a ventriloquist she reads its silent lip,
Interpreting the gnomic bubbles of its word,
Which bloop like quavers of a psychedelic trip,
Or nimble foldings of the origami bird.

As a surface of the pool begins to ripple,
She undoes the couplets of her blue kimono,
And as King Fish comes up, she offers him her nipple.

This, Dear Sir, is when the spirit enters matter
Or, as a master summarized it long ago,
Old pond: a frog jumps in: the sound of water.

Fuji Film

I feared the yen was starting to decline again,
Devaluing my take-home honorarium.
I joined the crowd that swarmed beneath the acid rain
Like schools of fishes in a vast aquarium.

Some wore sharkskin suits that shimmered like a rainbow;
Some were surgeons, with a white mask where their mouth should be;
Some bore barracuda grins, and some wore minnow;
One fat businessman swam like a manatee.

I saw two lobster samurai produce their swords
Of infinitely hammered folded Zeno steel,
That glittered like the icy blue of Northern fjords.

I snapped them slashing floating dollar bills in half
Beneath the signs for Coke, the giant neon roulette wheel,
The money index pulsing like a cardiograph.

Banana Tree

The President is bringing many things to mind
By gazing at the cherry-blossom as it blooms:
Dead young samurai; the harvest moon; a drawn blind;
Stiletto tilt of footsteps in deserted rooms.

This road: no going-person on it; twilight falls:
The President is listening for the temple bell,
And as she hears the frog splash in the holy well,
June rain's still falling through the roofs of marble halls.

And now the cherry blossom's blown from the bough—
Snow that we two looked at, did it fall again this year?—
The President divests herself of here and now

And transubstantiates herself into a swan,
Which disappears into a higher atmosphere:
Full moon: a walk around the pond; the night is gone.

February Fourteen

Meanwhile, back in Japan, it is Valentine's Day.
The love hotels are fully booked as Bethlehem,
As, canted like a drunken boulevardier,
My soul roams Tokyo holding one rose by its stem.

Snow is falling in the print by Hiroshige
That I gaze at in a hundred TV screens;
Bronze temple-gongs reverberate their cloisonée;
The light is orange-syncopated reds and greens.

Then I met you, Irish exiles, in the Fish Bar,
Where we staggered between three wobbly shamrock stools
Eyed by prismed species pouting in their glazed bazaar.

Fourteen Bloody Marys later you lisped of home.
We then discovered we had come from different schools,
Yet thought the same, like mutants of one chromosome.

from **Belfast Confetti: Haiku versions**

Plains and mountains, skies
all up to their eyes in snow:
nothing to be seen.
     —Joso

As a scarecrow blows
over: the first whispering
of the autumn wind.
                    —Kyoruku

I know the wild geese
ate my barley—yesterday?
Today? Where did they go?
                    —Yasui

To Lord Toba's hall
five or six horsemen blow in:
storm-wind of the fall.
                    —Buson

These are wild slow days,
echoes trickling in from all
around Kyoto.
                    —Buson

I've put on this
borrowed armour: second-hand
cold freezes my bones.
                    —Buson

In Kyoto, still
longing for Kyoto: cuck-
oo's two time-worn notes.
    —Bashō

⁓

Darkness never flows
except down by the river:
shimmering fireflies.
    —Chiyo

⁓

Eleven horsemen—
not one of them turns his head—
through the wind-blown snow.
    —Shiki

⁓

Wild rough seas tonight:
yawning over Sado Isle,
snowy galaxies.
    —Bashō

DEIRDRE CARTMILL

Karaoke in the Glasshouse

The ritual begins on my knees on the cold tiles,
the slow in and out, retching in darkness.
I flush the stains, flee to my local,
a glass-fronted victim of the new Belfast
where mosaic shopfronts no longer shatter
in a starshower of razor-edged reflections.
The Harp still tastes reliably bitter;
I drop to the bottom of a puddle of slops,

come up for air, watch the Karaoke clowns
force fifteen minutes fame from three minute wails.
Fatboy Slim spins on the jukebox
as the strobes colourwash me into a Warhol cameo.
I spy a wink, or an eyelid collapsing
under pellets of caked black mascara.
She squeezes past so close that her breath
slaps my face. I say nothing, get a hard-on.

I've been there before and know how the song ends
—everyone sing along now, play soldier,
elicit her name, where she's going to, coming from,
tell her you're sure you've met somewhere before,
loosen laughter with Bacardi Breezers,
chant second-hand stories, then shimmy to the Gents
and slip out the back door. It's simpler that way,
no embarrassed fumblings at last orders.

I'm under surveillance from too many lost souls,
remembering when they were flesh and touched my flesh.
I sang an unholy duet with the banshee—
when you flirt with death's girl, there's no room for regrets.
The glass eyes fatten my reflection.
I hang in limbo in a hall of mirrors,
two-faced, half way to a peaceful universe;
I click my heels and stagger homewards

to kneel alone in the midnight silence,
savour the short staccato spasms
as I ease my fingers down my warm throat,
move them in and out, in and out, faster now.
I fade from neon to ultraviolet,
watch dust motes circling in the jaundiced streetlight
that spills through the damp-ridden nets
on the window that's painted shut.

JUANITA CASEY

Zen and Now

Reading Bashō
Under fox-shared bracken,
Warblers distilling song
Out of early morning rain
And three swans pulsing
For a silver landfall;
That would please him—
Who'd have thought
Swans farted—
Plop!
The old pond and that famous frog...
Now we hear
It's a wrong translation.
Plop! an illusion.
Illustration: a buffalo,
Horned like a boomerang,
Carrying Grandpa
Rump-perched like a tinker;
In another, facing backward,
(All Desire Gone)
Like a kid on an obliging donkey.
A blank page—
'The Cow and Sage Quite Gone Out of Sight'...
Round the bend
Or through the gate,
The last water-buffalo
(With or without Sage),

The hundred Pythagorean oxen—
(The I-Ching: 'No Blame')
Or Mullingar heifer—
The cows of the world
Are the same;
Huffing strings of drooling effs,
Blatting flies with sinewy
Kelp-tails,
Pocketing the World
Through half-mast, megaphone ears,
And roundly gathering it in
With fish-bowl stares
Through gobstopper eyeballs;
'Quite out of Sight'?
Philosophy
Has forgotten the inevitable
Cowpat.

AUSTIN CLARKE

Japanese Print

Both skyed
In south-west wind beyond
Poplar and fir-tree, swallow,
Heron, almost collide,
Swerve
With a rapid
Dip of wing, flap,
Each in an opposite curve,
Fork-tail, long neck outstretched
And feet. All happened
Above my head. The pair
Was disappearing. Say I
Had seen, half hint, a sketch on
Rice-coloured air,
Sharako, Hokusai!

PATRICK COTTER

A Richard Brautigan Moment

"Are you writing a new poem?" said the Japanese girl
 her hair shimmering like a dark undiscovered continent.

I'm trying, musing over odd vacant imaginings,
distracted by the jungle beat of the bar's soundtrack
which shakes the potted palm leaves by my side.
"I'm trying," I say, above the underfed baby's wails.
Sometimes the words come more easily here
than in a silent room. The indiscernible voices,
multiple exhalations, clattering of glass and cups,
if not inspirational, are at least companionable,
making the great trek through the word-veldt
less lonesome. Maybe I should have said all this
rather than just "I'm trying".

What I said turned her round like a self-correcting,
Sony robotic puppy hitting the skirting board.

YVONNE CULLEN

Kabuki

Your old words lean tips of flame towards me
                      sometimes. They
line walls, with the thoughts
                      of shadow lamps;
can be light: back, like a level look from hills:
                      your meaning: joy. Joy:
what can be, with the man I love here.

And someone will step forward
                      sometimes.
On a Sunday on T.V, the Kabuki actor say he will try
                      to dance love and mourning:
love—not physical, though that will be in it, and
                      the dubbed voices say for us: love
most like the love between a human
                      and a bird that rests near them.

Small thing so true: it settles in my life—
                      on you, where you are, there:
we live it this lightly. And there's a night, when with
                      my French, your English, we
fix human importance
                      "alongside dead flies!";
resolve the world (even Bach) to one of those "things like an
                      upside—down glass"
whose domed shape loved hands would make,
                      whose snow they would have fall

with loved fingers, so I'd peel a life from myself
                            to accompany the life you'd have,
I'd reach out—my shy hand on your head—
                            believe you keep it.

TONY CURTIS

Siren Off Inisheer

A Japanese kimono seemed out of place
in the draughty three roomed cottage
sunk into the back of Inisheer, but
there you were, breasts tucked like
oranges in the colourful soft silk.

You arched your back and a shy ghost
lifted the kimono off your shoulders,
it slid to the floor and you were gone.
Through the small cruciform window
I shivered as you plunged and surfaced

like a seal a few yards beyond the rocks.
Then I noticed the caps rising on the pier.
The eyes of the three women by the front wall.
I could hear your siren's call from the sea.
I lifted your kimono and the latch off the door.

Northern Haiku

On an Antrim bog
a wall divides the wet land,
planted in the past.

Shot twice in the head.
Once in each astonished eye.
History is blind

Over the dark Foyle
the bark of Kalashnikovs,
an old Derry air.

Punishment shooting.
Pleads remorse and forgiveness.
Jeans gone at the knees.

Protestant prayers.
Popish prayers. Funerals.
We go the same way.

A man ploughing,
in one field he furrows from
Ireland to England.

A blackbird's sweet song
lost in the wildness of hills—
prayer for the dead.

Seven Haiku for Sahoko's Drawing

Stillness

Here is my stillness
light as Japanese maple—
falling in autumn.

Work

I work in this field,
the woman you see helps me—
it's all in the hands.

Fall

Before last night's storm
earth was clothed in green leaf—
now all has fallen.

Moon

When I wear my skin
I pull it tight as a coat—
lie still as the moon.

Snow

You spoke of crossing,
of leaving before the snows—
there's no sign of you.

Less

Down to the whiteness
my hands, my feet hold on to
less and less and less.

Autumn

Dreamt in October,
this is Sahoko's drawing—
autumn unveiling.

GERALD DAWE

The Moon Viewing Room

for Andy Fitzsimons

Johnny in Carroll's Bar shouts
'Two pies, one direct' as snow
falls like dust over Smithfield.
Up in the corner on the big TV,
moon man, lunatic, space cadet,
beams all the way in black
and white to our moon viewing.

Then, many moons after, in a temple
in Kyoto, on a little bridge from
here to eternity, as psychedelic
carp gawp in such a perfect pond,
rain spindled down the lattice work
gutter, and I too looked up
and saw the moon viewing room,

the turret open at each side,
for shogun, priest and poet
to visit and sit and watch the moon,
with only the device of a cloudless
sky, perhaps the snow falling also,
and the music of an icy stream.

Now I have it, at my attic window,
at whatever time it may be,
all at once, I see the snow that
will not last, the voice of a man
in his prime and the jabber of us all
in the crowded moon viewing room.

PATRICK DEELEY

Bashō on the Dodder

Whirligig beetle,
trout, swan—the brook's
growing pains.

My face laughs
where water's skin
isn't broken.

Moss living on moss
fossils. Keepsakes of water,
water spoken for.

Give of branches.
I tap this
rag tree, poetry.

Sudden thrush
sets foot; lizard scribbles
a goodbye note.

Wind jostles
the thin poplar. Patience
leans on a stick.

I unfurl
the leaf. A prescription
of nature's.

Mess of wild
fruit, my joy
the sorrowing plum.

Heron holds still,
a beard of minnows swaying
under his chin.

He's taken to
lighting on a street-lamp—
scout of sunset, neon.

No real standoff—
himself here, her nibs over
next the waterfall.

Juggernaut—
look! Scattered feathers,
an upset branch.

Leather-winged bat,
spinning darkness
on darkness.

Bed of sour stones,
the river's sweethearts
all in a flap.

Scrapings
and whistles—old mother's
bones, her breath.

I sleep out;
the promised wind
comes to sweep my roof.

GREG DELANTY

The Speakeasy Oath

to Liam Ó Muirthile

You borrowed my kimono with Japanese prints and verse
 legends of the soul's struggles,
its script more readable than the serif characters of our
 tattered Irish primers.
As you boiled water for the magic brew of Barry's tea,
 the Cork ginseng, to kick-start the day,
the kimono's druid sleeves, trailing across the stove,
 hey-presto caught fire.

Being still out for the count, I was startled awake by you
 raising the roof, ullagoning,
having a conniption, a canary, bellising 'Táim trí thine',
 'Fuck' 'Brostaigh', 'Bollox',
and a veritable string of swear words right out of the lost
 lexicon of old Irish oaths.
I vaulted out and tore into the kitchen without a stitch on.
 You were berilling
and back-berilling, in a mighty foster, like some stepdancer
 gone bonkers, lepping out a new berserk dance.

I got into the act, an bhriogáid dóiteáin, flaking the flaming
 sleeve, dousing
us pair of prancing artists with the kettle's hot water; me in
 me scald, dancing buff;

my willy, micky, connihaly, langer, crown jewels, one-eyed
    baldy man, thingamajig keeping time to the fire jig.
No sooner had we caught breath than we fell on the floor
    in stitches. A chara,
you yammered in between guffaws that it was a sign,
    a thumbs-up from the muses,
after our night before's oath to set the poetry world on fire
    while Big Joe Burrell, an fear gorm, blithely blues-sang.

Your Irish and my darned Cork-English airishin dipped
    and rose like the smoke in the yuppy Dockside,
the closest we could get to our mythical speakeasy
    with the New York mountains
across the lake leapfrogging each other into the dark
    eternity of America.

MOYRA DONALDSON

Kobi

a found poem

We were making the final preparations
for the New Year Tea Ceremony,
when the earth leapt up with a sound like doom.
We have a saying—
if a thing happens twice, it will happen again.

Bamboo

Knows how to make use of hollowness,
knows how to be insubstantial,
gives way, sways and bends,
is seldom broken ...

food paper book pipe mast
bucket fence thatch raft
medicine scaffolding
chopstick furniture

Carp

Success never closes
its eyes, never
stops swimming.

KATIE DONOVAN

Blossom Time

Tokyo, April 1995

Crown of blood-orange,
and the sun comes up electric,
shearing off the woolly cloud;

a procession of brides
is floating down the hill,
arms held out,
heads held high
with veils of pale pink,
and trimmings
of wakening birds.

All day the pilgrims gather
to pay homage; all day
the brides pose,
delicate in their finery.
I wander beneath
their rapturous milk rose sprays,
confetti of petal
softening in my hair.

Dusk comes, bruise-coloured,
and the nymphs
take up their night poses
beneath my window,

fists of flowers
holding off the rain.
They pinken my dreams
with cherry lace and sap,
underskirt of leaf;

morning finds my plodding body
fragrant and aflutter,
and I come up molten
with the sun.

MARY DORCEY

Grace

When you turn
your back
to me—
back comes

The first day
to me.
The first
time

I loved you
and saw
that long line
sweep

From shoulder
to flank.
As in
Japanese

Calligraphy—
one brush
stroke,
defining—

A precise
statement
of
grace.

KATHERINE DUFFY

Nightingales of the Little Emperors

Quiet, in vast, dark playgrounds,
the emperors' nightingales wait,
mentally rehearsing simulated songs,
flexing brittle wings
against extinction.

From wide glass cages
come the little emperors.
Lords of the first world, they
have imperious need of novelty;
they suffer a want of miracles.
They've got the tickets in their pockets.

The little emperors file on gingerly.
The metal birds, humming ominously,
consume them gently, and begin to tilt and sing.

SEAN DUNNE

The Frail Sprig

for Idit

The night is freezing hard. Frost
stiffens grass where I walk and watch
a full moon rising over our small, lost
planet no saviour now can touch.

You pose in blue in a photograph
set near my table and its waiting reams.
The dark floss of your hair enfolds
a face where smiles and hurt combine.

You look like one who knows the worth
of holding on or letting go.
Aglish, Roanmore, Dunhill, Gaultier,
I set my names against those you know:

Tiberias, Sinai, Beersheva, 'Amir.
When you were playing among the screams
of a six-day war, and begging to sleep
in bomb shelters as if dreams

might filter through trembling ground,
I burrowed in books in provincial streets.
Now, I trample hurt: a mound
where you lie waiting as I need

to leave pain behind, the used
chrysalis that yields a butterfly.
You haunt my movement like a muse.
Tonight I read Neruda, a wish unfurled:

'I want to do with you what Spring
does with the cherry blossom'—a dream
from our shared Japan and its snow
over leaves afloat on streams

where water is smooth as a kimono.
Against the night that's set in cold,
I place this frail sprig like a bowl
before a shrine. May it last and grow.

The Art of Tea

LEAVES

Let them be creased
like a horseman's boot,
curled like the dewlap
of a bullock.
Let them unfold
like mist in a ravine,
turn wet and soft
like earth rinsed with rain.

CUP

The blue glaze
of southern jade:
the perfect hollow
of a teacup.

Stir with
a bamboo whisk.
Drink and feel
the soul flood.

BOILING

Bubbles begin:
the eyes of fishes.
Bubbles swell:
crystals in a pool.
Bubbles burst:
waves in a storm.

TEA ROOM

Let it be solitary
as a cottage on a beach.
Let no sword sully
this abode of vacancy.
With linen napkin
and bamboo dipper,
let it be a shrine
for the ordinary,
for talk of tea

and the taking of tea,
best made with water
from a mountain spring.

A Shrine for Lafcadio Hearn, 1850-1904

Like an artist painting on rice-grains,
he tried to trap Japan in a story:
his one good eye so close to the page
he might have been a jeweller with a gem.

So much to tell: kimonos and cranes,
cemeteries to stalk at evening, slow
shoals of candles—souls
on rivers beneath a massive moon.

Even the sound of sandals on a bridge
stayed in the mind for an evening,
matching the shadow of fishermen
on still waters: a painted print.

Or a face smiling to hide its grief,
the touch of passing sleeves
part of a plan that maps the future,
a heron seeking the heights on a wall.

Loneliness ended in Matsue: that raw
pain no longer gnawing like the Creole
songs on a sidewalk in New Orleans.
Instead he heard a flute's clear note.

He was a lantern drifting from the shore,
dissolving in the tone of a struck bell.
Sipping green tea in Tokyo, he heard
ghost stories from an impossible past

and died past fifty from his Western heart.
Afterwards, he was a story still told, set
firmly as rocks in a Zen garden.
Incense burns near cake at his shrine.

In the sound of sandals on a bridge
I hear him sometimes, or catch him
In the swift calligraphy of a scroll,
or in the curve of a rough bowl.

A breeze through a bamboo-grove,
his memory passes for an instant.
Snow falls on his grave and on plum-blossom.
He is fading like a fisherman in mist.

Shiatsu Sequence

SHOES

As if before a temple,
I leave my shoes outside:
clutter in a corner,
cares that I discard.

THE MAT

I press my face against it,
its smell of herbs and oil:
a pattern rich with potions,
stories it's absorbed.

CHIMES

Cylinders wait for the wind
to claim their metal song.
Watching them, I wait for you
to free hurt like a bird.

KNOTS

Muscles ease at your touch,
nets of knots you discover.
You work until they open:
a mother loosening laces.

TEARS

Tears pour as if a prophet
tapped a rock with a stick.
You draw them out: threads
to twist in comfort's rug.

OIL

Its smell fills the room,
a rattle of jars and bowls.
The sound of it pouring:
milk from tiny teats.

SCARF

A heron flashes from reeds
and grips the fish in a pool.
It is over: your peace a scarf
in which my cares lie bundled.

PAUL DURCAN

Wild Sports of Japan

to Mamoru Odajima and Michiko Wakamatsu

That snow-bound January we spent
Shooting motor cars in northern Japan
In one short afternoon
I bagged five Mitsubishi and one Nissan.

6.30 a.m., 13 January 2004, Hokkaido Prefecture

Human beings are peculiar creatures which is why we cranes—
We red-crested Japanese cranes—
Congregate at daybreak in the shallow bend of the river
To shoot video of human beings on the red bridge.

Raftery in Tokyo

Suicidal in Tokyo,
A crow on a telegraph pole
Raucous with self-pity,
Ah, ah, ah—I squawk.

From County Mayo to Greater Tokyo
Men with failing eyesight go
Serenading that crazy innocence
They see because they know.

The Journey Home from Japan

The hard part of the journey home
To Ireland from Japan
Is not the fourteen hours in the air
Nor the bumps in the ceilings
Between Mongolia and Siberia
Nor when over Norway the pilot drawls
"Boys and girls—glad you're still with us"
Nor the maze of Heathrow
Nor the rat-run of the London-Dublin flight
Nor the cave-light of Dublin Airport.
The hard part,
Having stumbled from the taxi
And fumbled with the key in the door,
Is facing into my place
Smelling of droppings of suicide.
At least back in Japan
Suicide is an honourable end,
Not like in Ireland
A furtive act of disgrace.

Facing Extinction

to Masazumi Toraiwa

When I rounded the corner into Anne Street
And I was confronted by a man squatting in a doorway
I got a shock and I flinched.
For the face I saw was the same face
I saw in the shaving mirror this morning.

Dropping my ludicrous lucre into his beaker
I squeaked: "Are you all right?"
He announced: "I think I'm going to be all right."
And he proffered me a smile, looking me straight in the eye.

I crossed over into Chatham Street
And I slipped into The Great Outdoors
Where I purchased a pair of walking shoes—
Brasher Hillmasters—
Having been instructed last week in northern Hokkaido
By a samurai-ninja protector of bears—
Brown bears facing extinction—
That the time was nigh
For me to face the truth about my fellow creatures.

On my way back along Anne Street
There was a different man in the same doorway
Looking more doomed than the first man—
More doomed to extinction—
His head bowed as if in meditation on death.
Dropping my ludicrous lucre into his beaker
I squeaked: "Are you all right?"
He announced: "I'm fine—how are you?"
And he proffered me a smile, looking me straight in the eye.

In my cave on the edge of the city
A woman on the telephone mocks me:
"You were always a bear"
As if I *should / could* have been somebody else.
Peering again into my shaving mirror
At my bear's eyes, my bear's mouth,
I am surprised by how upbeat, yet melancholy, I look:
In the autumn of my days I am looking forward
To hibernation, facing extinction.

DESMOND EGAN

Hiroshima

for Akira Yasukawa

Hiroshima your shadow burns
into the granite of history

preserves for us pilgrims
a wide serious space
where one may weep in silence

I carry in my mind
a glass bullet lodged deep
the memory of that epicentre where
one hundred thousand souls
fused at an instant

and the picture of a soldier
tenderly offering a cup of water
to a burnt child who cannot respond

the delicate paper cranes*

---

* folded paper birds left by children at the Children's Monument

JOHN ENNIS

Watching the Descent of Yuichiro Miura
first to ski down the top of Everest

Miura, alone in a tent of candles, desolate at heart,
You wait for dawn on Everest, the challenge of Icarus.
World champion, skier of the fastness of our high sky
Your meekness is etched forever on the peerless glacier.
O pilgrim, these high peaks pirate away your identity
As the frigid pavilion of the mountain becomes a tomb.
Brain cells deteriorate. All the warm human senses dull.
Ice walls lighten to pools of silver in the western coomb.

At these heights, a universe of silence. Imagination is
Eclipsed and the mind exhausts the last squirrel stores
Of cognisance. At twenty thousand feet, the south coll
Trails its royal plumes of snow down to the jet stream.
Yesterday, on your last trial, a loss of consciousness:
Parachute on the sacred sheer like an airy lotus blossom.
The frozen dome was too brittle even for the brave Sherpas.
One died. But guides would not allow you call off the climb.

The Himalayan partridge spreads her wings many miles below
Where meadowed valleys speak with rivulets, honeyed wells.
Up here, the ozone is no more than a stone's throw
From Yeats's cold fisherman by his river in the hills.
The grey guinea-pigs of industry this morning at home
Motor the daily labyrinths of steel, tooth and claw.
This older firmament holds the same vitreous chrome.
Frozen outcrops jut up tall as ten Liberty Halls.

Higher, where the Swedes stopped, two thousand cold feet
From the actual summit, you ascend totally at your ease.
The day is eerie with freezing. Grit of névé blasts cheek
Bones. Zero here is tropical. The icebox never thaws.
Oxygen starts to sing, deeper now, rehearsed in your lungs.
You're so high the sky is blackening! Crevasses crowd
Commonplace! One false step on the fickle snow of words…
Peaks are puny abutments into a dark deep nothingness.

Blur! Hunch of granular! You are off! Ski the glacier,—
Attempt the unknown packed aeons of our primal Everest,
Hug her rock-strewn slalom. Your split-second diagonals
Confirm a hold on the white Pegasus of the mountain!
If arms were wings you would be Greek, daring Icarus.
The earth and sky are yours and God's white thigh of myth.
You play with the ondes martinou every frenzy of style
Redeeming all prose voices buried deep in the ancient rime.

Poet, with a plummeting of skis, steel nerve, leaden skies
You somersault. Sherpas of dismay strike out for your body's
Mad cascade just halted at the black rock, the white abyss.
Telescopic eyes rivet on your soul where you lie unharmed.
As you weep, I think of those few humans to court greatness,
Embrace your humility and courage beneath the pewter sky
And your noble art shooting the last rapids of space,
Apices of ice to whose state you bring illumination.

Miura, you had feared the old gods of the sun,
Moon, and the far off white extinguishable stars
As fated as those colourful Tibetan villagers
Begging you to join their dance at a festival.
You walk down from a high wind crying in summer,
From the cairn of thanks you built the Mountain,
Child of the sea, altar with a mirror to honour
Her, beautiful among her sisters at the top of the world.

PETER FALLON

World Peace

Cherries like ours
on their cherry tree.

Rock islands
in a gravel sea.

> *Ryōan-ji Temple, Kyoto*

GERARD FANNING

Week-end Away

Running the lexicon of cold and thaw
our hotel whinnies in its vatic store.

Go on, croon your weird music,
I'll hum the cantata from a Japanese opera,

and like shy samurai
we'll leave this world with a cosy virus

clutching a jar of wild honey
to nourish our sleep in the ocean.

And should we drown in our own fluid
and our almanac of phrases

unravel the signature of influenza,
let the helix of clefs and quavers—

embalmers script in Indian ink—
compose our spirited gavotte.

ANDREW FITZSIMONS

after Kenkō's Essays in Idleness

Worlds

Travel. Wherever you go
the world you bring with you
is washed by the world you see.

The Risen Tide

Impermanent is the risen tide.
Yesterday's pools, tomorrow's puddles.
Exeunt omnes. Tempus fugit.

What does day teach the day?
The peach and damson trees
in the garden will not say.

The Autumn Night

I pass the long autumn nights
tearing up old notes and letters,
putting the afterlife in order;
word by word,
self upon dishevelled self remembered.
And then I light upon
a dead friend's thoughts
and somewhere a high door opens

and I am silent, stared at,
by night, by dawn.

A Letter

On a morning of snow I wrote a letter.
"And how could you write and not mention the snow?"
Dear friend, long departed, it is snowing again.

Ornaments

What is bad taste?
too many knick-knacks about the place
too many brushes in the ink-box
too many Buddhas
too many shrubs and plants in a garden
too many rooms in a house
too many words on meeting someone
a ledger all plus and no minus?

The Human

This business of life, getting on—
like making a snowman in Spring:
scrimshawed stones, brassoed buttons,
that touch of the human,
and a soundless dripping within.

Shunkashūto

Spring

In Herbert Park under a cherry tree
we improvise a Spring Ceremony:
cream crackers for rice snacks;
for *sake*? Irish whiskey.

Summer

We have come to Asagaya
to watch the locals dance *bon-odori*.
When the heavens break
and open, told you so, you say.

Autumn

Lake Chuzenji. Maple leaves
dyed by a wine-red hand,
finished off by us, our car.

Winter

The New Year Samurai-soap this year:
Miyamoto Musashi, his life and loves,
though why to the sounds of Ireland?

ANTHONY GLAVIN

from *Living in Hiroshima*

Ground Zero

Morbid incandescence. I snap awake.
A warhead, sky high? No, you're standing there,

Flashing your Instamatic, grinning. I freak.
How should I ever bring home to you the horror?

Magic!

Thunder like Mt. Fuji swallowing itself alive.
A bicycle sagged and melted in its own shadow.

Stones bled. Birds fell roasted out of the sky.
We just stood there, helpless. You can't hate magic.

Aioi Bridge

Slime-strips of skin that flapped like seaweed,
No mouths, no noses, eyeless, faceless, screaming,

They dived in hundreds off the twisted girders.
The river was warm and merciful. It killed quickly.

A Month Early

Even then I must have raged at being confined.
But to push for freedom *that* Bank Holiday weekend!

My father homing from Youghal in his chrome V8
To hold my mother, then me, then celebrate....

Nostalgia

What once so bright now starts to fade and blur
As we are closed-out by our memories—

But oh! such lightfall, such idyllic skies
That summer before... before it all... before...

The Domei News Agency

HQ reacted swiftly to reports
That rumours of 'Atom Sickness' had reached the West—

The Domei Agency was ordered closed.
Such is the use of silence. Silence aborts.

Museum Time

Fused *sake* cups, blent watches, melt-lumped coins—
And nothing we can ever learn from them

But rage and outrage fixed in a half-life aftersilence
Where the time is always 8.16 a.m.

MARK GRANIER

The Great Wave—Hokusai

Whatever ocean we broke from—
navy and ice-blue rollers
snowballing spume—

freeze-frames, as the world's
coral-fingered wave
whelms and cradles

slim, reed-coloured boats
(inset with fragile fishermen
bald as pearls) unsinkable

as Fuji poking into
or out of the blue its
frosted fin.

PAMELA GREENE

Waiting for You

I have put on a Japanese face,
combed camellia oil into my hair
and poured green tea into two tiny cups
fragile as rice paper.

I am kneeling on the tatami matting
in my blue and green kimono
with obi of crimson,
your favourite colours.

To pass the time, I paint ideographs
on a silk screen;
your name,
over and over,
as though in naming you
I could capture the youness of you.

And if I could recreate you, flesh and bone,
would you be as you were
or would you be a stranger
because my memory has failed
to preserve you perfectly?

How long the night is.
I sit with hands resting one in the other
as you taught me,
though decorum was never an easy lesson.

The wind rises.
You will not come now
and tomorrow the cherry blossom
will shed its petals, one by one.

EAMON GRENNAN

Sunshine, Salvation, Drying Shirt

Between the big window and the lake's blind flashes
I hang my line of Sunday washing—most of it grey
or black, one shirt ecclesiastical white, so you'd think
a priest was tucked away here off the beaten track
where—perched on the cross of the ESB pole—a kestrel
fills my head with Hopkins and his windhover
which I caught the other evening standing on air
unbuckled, almost stopped there, so I could spot
when the bird tilted—silhouetting itself—the crucifix
the poet must have seen, a sign bringing Christ
into the picture, causing the creature to buckle and
give off blood and fire, making a holy show of itself.

Flies hum, skiving a shaft of sunshine, and a chaffinch
dabs at the bread I shared with him for breakfast: could I
have been, I wonder, a monk of the Ninth Century,
my heart, too, in hiding, *stirred for a bird* and finding
God's fingerprints on everything? Drowsing outside,
the book of Bashō fallen from my lap, I hear the note
a chaffinch makes breaking day in half, then gone, then
another answering with a little run of song, then silence
as the summer air lets go of them, teaching us how.
In his cell, the monk bends to scratch his ankle, watch
an ant at work, or opens the door to take the day to heart,
as, in a word-flurry, Father Hopkins blesses himself
before his bird can terminate its dive and take the life of
something hidden in the grass—a mouse, a lark—stabbing

through the neck and biting its head off. Meantime,
sun's a wonder on the back of my hand, my splayed shirts
keep shadow-boxing on the line, and a million midges dance
like dervish angels on a pinhead of light. When such days
stretch their slow-burning bodies out for us, it's hard to believe
the incredible weather won't hold up, as we want it to,
forever. But it won't, and even in the middle of its comforts
I know the flies gyring my head like atomies of air
would, given half a chance, make a quick meal of these
pulpy eyes. Still, with the last cleansing drop dripped out,
my clothes grow lighter in the light breeze, becoming
crisp as souls new-shriven, and from high in the heavens'
cloudless blue comes a twangy drumming as a snipe
shows off its climbing power—its silvered body all
bat-flap and ascension against the open sky—then turn
and curve, twist and fall, angling its tail-feathers to
make music from its own body falling like that, as if
singing the risk itself for the frightful pleasure of it.

Near Mount Kurokami, Bashō changed apparel and his name,
then stood behind a waterfall and looked straight out
at what kept going. Next daybreak he was *off again
on unknown paths*. Here, pinned to its place, my white shirt
is all puffed up, I see, with its own radiance—a full sail
going nowhere—and in this silence that's come down on us
now towards evening like a cloud of light, the iron sound
of the Angelus bell beats round and round the valley.

MAURICE HARMON

Japanese Garden

```
            HILL NORTH     BLACK TURTLE     THREE CYPRESSES
 M                                                                S
 A      azaleas             pruned          to mountain peaks     T
 P                                                                R
 L          stones    in                    attitudes             E
 E                                                                A
 S                                                                M
                        arranged
 S                                                                E
 E                                                                A
 V                                                                S
 E                                  disarranged                   T
 N

 T                                                                B
 I                                                                L
 G      take heart                                                U
 E                                                                E
 R
                                                                  D
                                                                  R
                                    where two roads cross         A
 W                                                                G
 H                                                                O
 I      and four roads join                                       N
 T
 E                       black
                                                                  N
                                                                  I
 W                                                                N
 E                                                     red        E
 S                                           blue
 T                                                                W
                                                                  I
                                                                  L
 P          white                                                 L
 A                                                                O
 T                                                                W
 H                                                                S
            POND SOUTH      CRIMSON BIRD    NINE JUDAS
```

Afternoon Tea

We have come a long way for this:
the music building with its vane trumpeter,

the fluent stream, the plenitude of webs
in the low-sized evergreens,

our tea ceremony under the trees
beside the lacecap hydrangeas.

By local lore we do not do it right,
but I love the eager way you bring out

the latest batch of rock buns,
or the plate of hot buttered scones.

The water, you say, must be piping hot,
the pot scalded, the tea drawn.

We've done it this way for years.
I may not sweep the path,

or sprinkle water on stone,
but my heart bows to you.

MICHAEL HARTNETT

from *Inchicore Haiku*

1
Now, in Inchicore,
my cigarette-smoke rises—
like lonesome pub-talk.

6
No goldfinches here—
puffed sparrows in sunpatches
like Dublin urchins.

8
My English dam bursts
and out stroll all my bastards.
Irish shakes its head.

11
On a brick chimney
I can see all West Limerick
in a jackdaw's eye.

17
Songs from my young days
and high spirits in small towns—
ash floats in the air.

19
In local chippers
sad cod dream in fresh batter.
The Atlantic cries.

30
The cats at civil war
in the partitioned garden.
I stroke my whiskers.

32
A pint of Guinness—
black as my Catholic heart,
black as broken vows.

40
Dead faces watch me—
people I have wronged and loved.
Milk sours in the cup.

59
The warm dead go by
in mahogany boxes.
'They're well-housed at last.'

67
In local chippers,
queueing for carbohydrates—
a dwarfed people.

78
On Tyrconnell Road,
Catholic Emancipation—
thirteen milk-bottles.

FRANCIS HARVEY

A Tanka and Four Haiku

Your cold white hands that
cage this huge crucifix once
caged me with love but
why does that bird outside beat
against the corpse-room window?

Why am I afraid
to open this silver box
full of a child's hair?

Why do you sigh in
your sleep? Why does the night wind
sigh in the aspen?

The dove hides in the
oak's shadow but who will hide
in the hawk's shadow?

The sapling quivers
after the bird has flown and
the hawk's craw is full.

SEAMUS HEANEY

1.1.87

Dangerous pavements.
But I face the ice this year
With my father's stick.

The Strand

The dotted line my father's ashplant made
On Sandymount Strand
Is something else the tide won't wash away.

Fiddleheads

Fiddlehead ferns are a delicacy where? Japan? Estonia? Ireland long ago?

I say Japan because when I think of those delicious things I think of my friend Toraiwa, and the surprise I felt when he asked me about the erotic. He said it belonged in poetry and he wanted more of it.

So here they are, Toraiwa, frilled, infolded, tenderized, in a little steaming basket, just for you.

Midnight Anvil

If I wasn't there
When Barney Devlin hammered
The midnight anvil
I can still hear it: twelve blows
Struck for the millennium.

His nephew heard it
In Edmonton, Alberta:
The cellular phone
Held high as a horse's ear,
Barney smiling to himself.

Afterwards I thought
Church bels beyond the starres heard
And then imagined
Barney putting it to me:
'You'll maybe write a poem.'

What I'll do instead
Is quote those waterburning
Medieval smiths:
'Huf, puf! Lus, bus! Col!' *Such noise
On nights heard no one never.*

And Eoghan Rua
Asking Séamus MacGearailt
To forge him a spade
Sharp, well shaped from the anvil,
And ringing *sweet as a bell.*

RACHAEL HEGARTY

There is No Love in Hykyu

Along the river
Called Liffey, leaves
Fall loudly.

In a Japanese
Town called Matsue,
Leaves fall.

Forgive me, my love,
I am forgetting our once
Shared language.

JOHN HEWITT

Gloss, on the Difficulties of Translation

Across Loch Laig
the yellow-billed blackbird
whistles from the blossomed whin.

Not, as you might expect,
a Japanese poem, although
it has the seventeen
syllables of the haiku.
Ninth-century Irish, in fact,
from a handbook on metrics,
the first written reference
to my native place.

In forty years of verse
I have not inched much further.
I may have matched the images;
but the intricate wordplay
of the original—assonance,
rime, alliteration—
is beyond my grasp.

To begin with, I should
have to substitute
golden for *yellow*
and *gorse* for *whin*,
this last is the word we use
on both sides of Belfast Lough.

JOHN HUGHES

Nagasaki

I arrive in the city
to sell the skull
of Saint Thomas Aquinas
to a retired policeman.

A passer-by tells me to panic.

I prise open the nearest door,
climb to the third floor,
and walk in on a geisha
listening to herself on the radio
describe how she navigated by the stars
out of her dead mother's womb.

She asks why she sweats blood
when I touch her where I shouldn't.

I wake up clinging onto
the second horseman of the Apocalypse
in his disguise as the tail-fin
of a high-altitude American bomber.

PEARSE HUTCHINSON

Sneachta i gCuach Airgid

Sneachta i gcuach airgid
níor líonas riamh ná ní fhacas
ach siúcra i mbabhla ómra
charnas i gcistin go minic

Siúcra bán
i mbabhla ómra

Dar le Zeami,
máistir Nó,
b'in an suaimhneas,
b'in sáimhe:
sneachta i gcuach airgid

Níl agam féin
ach babhla ómra
go siúcra geal
ach minic a líonaim
ómra go bruach
'gus cuirim ina seasamh ann
spúnóg airgid

Diaidh ar ndiaidh
titeann an spúnóg

Má chuirim ar ais í
ón gcupán tae
sa mbabhla ómra

Snow in a Silver Bowl

Snow in a silver bowl
I never heaped nor saw
but sugar into amber
often poured in a kitchen

White sugar
in an amber bowl

According to Zeami,
master of Noh,
that was stillness,
that was serenity:
snow in a silver bowl

White sugar
in amber glass
is all I've got
but often I fill
amber to the brim
and stand up in it
a silver spoon

Bit by bit
the spoon tilts

If I put it back
from the cup of tea
into the amber bowl

seans go seasfaidh
ach céard a cheapfadh
Zeami díomsa
dá gcuirfinn ar ais í
ón gcupán tae
i gcroí sciamhach an tsiúcra
sa tsneachta suaimhneach
gan í a thriomú
go dian mí-shuaimhneach?

Síocháin ar bith
níl ann gan aineamh
spúnóga airgid
as trousseau mo mháthar
dhíolas i bhfad ó shin
ar ór bocht gránna:
an spúnóg a sheasaim
i mbráid an tsneachta
i gcuach ómra
ghoid ar mo shon-sa
cara liom é
ón óstán is órga
in iarthar Eorpa

Bhí 'fhios aige go rabhamar
beo bocht ag an am úd:
ar éigean spúnóg bhréige
sa teach gan trácht ar airgead
ná sneachta i gcuach

Go tobann ón gcistin ghalánta
ar chistin na dáimhe boichte
thuirling spúnóga
greanta gréasta airgid

it may stand up
but what can Zeami
think of me
if I return it
from the cup of tea
to the lovely heart of sugar
to snow serenity
without even drying it
unserenely?

No tranquility
without a blemish
the silver spoons
from my mother's trousseau
I sold them long ago
for ugly brass:
the spoon I stand
in snowy breast
in amber glass
a friend liberated it
from the goldenest hotel
in the western world

He knew at the time
we were wretched-poor:
scarce even a phony spoon
let alone silver
or snow in a bowl

From the swanky kitchen
to the kitchen of poor poets
all of a sudden a cascade
of highly elaborate silver

Anois má fheicim
siúcra geal i mbabhla ómra
cuimhním ort, a Sheosaimh

Cuimhním ort ag sclábhaíocht
i gcistin shuarach an tsaibhris
cuimhním ar do bhlianta i ngéibheann
ar son na saoirse
        i gcéin, i ndeas,
ar son an tsuaimhnis
ar son na sáimhe
        i gcéin, i ndeas,
cuimhním ar do mhisneach do-chloíte
ar do mhisneach comh gleoite le sneachta

Now when I see white
sugar in the amber bowl
it's you I remember, Joe

I remember you slaving
in the wretched kitchen of wealth
I remember your years in prison
for the sake of freedom
        both near and far
in the cause of serenity
for the sake of stillness
        both near and far
I remember your courage unbeaten
your courage as handsome as snow

Koan

for William Cowper and Umberto Saba

Clearing a kitchen surface too long cluttered
you hear the sound
                      of spent matches
touching the handle of a silver spoon
a gentle tinkle
      you never heard
           that particular
sound before—
il mondo meraviglioso:
there's always a first time

Would unspent matches
lightly driven against
the handle of a silver spoon
make a different sound?

BIDDY JENKINSON

Tóraíocht Tai Haku *sna plandlannaí*

"*Prunus Tai Haku*
atá uaim,
silín mór bláthbhán na Seapáine,
silín an teampaill

Bláthóidh sé
i ndiaidh an draighin
i mbéal na sceach

Soilseoidh sé
duibhe seanfhraoigh
ruacht seanraithní
léithe seanchloch
guagacht Aibreáin

Tai Haku
led thoil."

"Fathach feá é
Níl éileamh ach ar abhaic phaitió
Ní bhfaighfidh tú é."

"*Prunus Tai Haku?*"
"*Amanogawa!*"

"*Prunus Tai Haiku?*"
"*Hokusai!*"

"*Prunus Tai Haiku?*"
"Agus fáilte!"

Smúdar, seanbhualtrach, leasú
ábhairín aoil, uisciú
clocha thart air
  á dhaingniú
ag bailiú drúchta
ag bac fiailí

Phléasc duilleoga ar dhath an umha
Chruinnigh bachlóga corcra
a sceith ina mbláthanna *pinc*

Leanas ag tál uisce ar an ruidín salach
mallacht i ngach braon uisce
in aghaidh an chnoic

An dé á choinneáil ann go fómhar
go gcaithfinn ar ais ag fear an tsiopa é
le "*Kanzan* ort
is ná raibh maith"

Ach tá frog tar éis seilbh a ghlacadh
ar an tamhnach faoi.
Suíonn sé ina chlochar úr i lár fhásach samhraidh
ag feitheamh ar a chandam laethúil uisce
á choisreacan.

FRED JOHNSTON

The Blue Whale

In the window of *The Blue Whale*
Faces of red clay pout and scowl,
And a tired girl pushes a pram up, up
The slope of the rue Rodier,
Walking slowly, almost elegant
In a blue-spotted dress and bare legs.

      Here is the house where Nogashima,
Tanka master, lived and wrote—read
His chiseled plaque. And just above it,
Leaning from a black wrought-iron balcony,
      A girl, bare-armed, with her hair
      Falling over her face,

      Appears to be waiting for someone.

EILEEN KATO

Sakurajima

Day-long unfolding
Its deep mountain mystery—
The untold beauty
Of all God's great works that hold
Inside them a heart of fire.
3rd April, 5:30 p.m

Is that rising trail
Of unlovely mouse-grey smoke
All you have to show
For the unquenchable fire
Raging deep within your heart?
4th April, 4:30 p.m.

Yesterday's dull plume
Is now a splendid panache,
A white cloud rising—
The changing changeless mountain
Shows its latest change of heart.
5th April, 2:30 p.m.

Note: Sakurajima is an island just off Kagoshima city formed of a volcanic mountain rising out of Kinkō bay.

NEVILLE KEERY

Far Away

Is the poetry group
meeting in Brussels?
Is that the thread
stretching to Japan
that pulls me out of bed
to write again?
The shock of the new is
re-interpreting what we know.

THOMAS KINSELLA

Old Harry

Death states the theme

'Master Love', my grim instructor assured me,
'Moved already in the criminal darkness
Before our dust was chosen, or choice began,

Devising—for spirits that would not fall asunder
At a touch—a flesh of thirst and pain, a blood
Driven by onward self-torment and by desire.'

'*What of the guilty spirit*', I inquired,
'*Inviting darkness to the human womb?*'
'The guilty must repay with flesh and blood.'

'*What of the innocent spirit, in pursuit
Of justice and the good?*' 'The innnocent
Repay with flesh and blood.' Then we proceeded.

The Twilight of Old Harry

Pink eyelids dipped in terror. Softly, possessed,
Voles flew like shuttles through the brush. A buzzard
Completed its loop of threat above the trees.

He marched with feeble vigour through the forest.
Down dappled levels of oak, alleys of beech,
Beams of sunlight flickered on his hide of tweed

And flared on his spectacles, two sightless coins.
In a quiet clearing, round a turn of the path,
He laid on a rich red tree his mottled hand

Who time and time again brought it down sharply
To put a stop, when he had cause, to anger,
The dangers of narrow thought, or mere habit,

So long ago... Assembled like steel children
Around his gleaming table they advised
And were absorbed, as he imposed reason

—A curb to the rash, a pupil to the wise.
Until on a certain day he waved them out,
Thoughtful before his maps. And chose at last

The greater terror for the lesser number.
With rounded cheeks he blew a moral blast
And the two chosen cities of the plain

Lost their flesh and blood—tiles, underwear, wild cries
Stripped away in gales of light. Lascivious streets
Heightened their rouge and welcomed baths of pure flame.

In broad daylight delicate creatures of love
Opened their thighs. Their breasts melted shyly
And bared the white bone. At that sight

Men blushed fiercely and became shades.
The air in a passion inhaled, and all dissolved
Or collapsed shimmering on black recesses,

A silken scenery of Heaven and Hell;
Exhaled, and the tympanum of earth shuddered,
Day cracked like a lantern and its blazing oils

Soared up in turmoil in thick vessels of dust.
Anthropophagi moaned in the buckling cloud,
Amazons and chimaerae, leaving the world.

Where once the cities of wickedness had stood
Eye sockets with nerves and ducts smouldering,
Moistened like two wells the plain's enamelled face.

A scrap of autumn silence came fluttering down
To touch his wrist with its invisible lace.
He shivered in golden light.

                              The scabby trunk
Broke the surface of his dream. He scratched
In vacant memory of mucous pleasure.

A nest of twittering naked animals.
Eyes clenched, grinning together in blind terror,
They tremble snout to snout, appearing to kiss.

A paw strokes a soft flank as though to comfort.
At each light touch a little blood enriches
The threads linking heart to heart and lip to lip.

MATT KIRKHAM

Unfinished Haiku

Every morning I drive along the shore
of Strangford Lough and sometimes it is clear
which is sky, which is sea, mountain, which sun,

and on other mornings the sea is where
the iron sky should be, there's a dragon
beneath the mountains and the car flies off
the gravity-loosened road, becomes the sun.

Shiko Munakata, woodblock artist,
chronically short-sighted, nose-heavy specs,
face so close to where his chisel became
the absence of wood he'd near breathe it in,

carved Wisdom, a monk trying to outstare
his own crossed and double-jointed fingers,
with a large hole in his cross-eyed head.

ANATOLY KUDRYAVITSKY

Unobana in Full Bloom

Haiku re-workings of poems from Daishoji Zen Convent, Kyoto

your colour is delight,
o flowering plum,
but now: your perfume!

    after Kazan (968—1008)

autumn wind…
I yearn for the place
from where it blows

    after Minamoto Masakane (1079—1143)

drenching myself,
I break off a spray of wisteria—
spring's end

    after Nakatsukasa, before 1265

pinks blooming
in divers shapes and hues—
the seeds all looked the same

    after Minamoto Chikamoto, before 1310

unobana in full bloom—
mountain cuckoo,
sing us into twilight

after Nijōin Sanuki, before 1320

snow-covered trees…
some of them evergreen;
which?

after anonymous poet, before 1470

deep into the summer,
a row of iris painting
its spring blooms

after Sanjōnishi Sanetaka (1455-1537)

autumn bamboo-grass—
Mount Icoma bedecked in white
already

after Arisugawa Yokihito (1656—1699)

crimson maple leaves,
our autumn hearts'
proper hue

after anonymous poet, before 1726

MICHAEL LONGLEY

A Gift of Boxes

I

Rice grains between my chopsticks remind you of a flower.
I want to wash the hagi petals in my bowl, then balance
Before your lips an offering of crabs' brains on a shiso leaf
Which looks like a nettle from Ireland but does not sting.

II

We are completely out of proportion in the tea-house
Until we arrange around a single earthenware bowl
Ourselves, the one life, one meeting, a ribbon of water
And these makeshift ideograms of wet leaves, green tea.

III

You make a gift of boxes by putting boxes inside
Boxes, each one containing the Japanese air you breathe,
More and more of it in diminishing boxes, smallness
Condensing in the end to two boxes the size of tears.

IV

They have planted stones in the stone garden. If I sit still
The stones will take root in my imagination and grow.
You retire behind the fifteenth stone which I cannot see.
Whatever happens to a stone becomes its life, its flower.

A Grain of Rice

Wrap my poem around your chopsticks to keep them clean.
I hardly know you. I do not want you to die. Our names
Fit on to a grain of rice like Hokusai's two sparrows,
Or else, like the praying mantis and the yellow butterfly,
We are a crowd in the garden where nothing grows but stones.
I do not understand the characters: sunlight through leaves,
An ivy pattern like fingers caressing a bowl, your face
In splinters where a carp kisses the moon, the waterfall
Up which its fins will spiral out of sight and into the sky.
Wrap my poem around your chopsticks to keep them clean.
Does it mean I shall not have taken one kiss for ever?
Your unimaginable breasts become the silkworm's shrine.

A Pair of Shoes

Who stole my shoes from the Garden of Ryoan-ji?
Have they come near you in Tokyo or Nagoya
Or Takayama? Fifteen rocks make up the landscape
We borrow, faraway places in gravelly sea.

The Weather in Japan

Makes bead curtains of the rain,
Of the mist a paper screen.

Birds and Flowers

for Fuyuji Tanigawa

My local The Chelsea where I took you for a pint
Has been demolished, which leaves us drinking in the rain,
Two inky smiles on handkerchiefs tied for luck like dolls
Flapping where the window should be, in Ireland or Japan.

A wagtail pauses among maple leaves turning from red
To pink in the picture you enclose with your good news:
'I have been a man of home these years,' you write, 'often
Surprised to know so much passion hidden in myself.'

You who translated for me 'ichigo-ichie' as 'one life,
One meeting' as though each encounter were once-in-a-
Lifetime, have been spending time with your little children:
'But I will go back to the world of letters soon.' Fuyuji,

The world of letters is a treacherous place. We are weak
And unstable. Let us float naked again in volcanic
Pools under the constellations and talk about babies.
The picture you sent to Belfast is called 'Birds & Flowers'.

White Water

in memory of James Simmons

Jimmy, you isolated yourself
At the last bend before white water.
We should have been fat jolly poets
In some oriental print who float
Cups of warm saké to one another
On the river, and launch in paper boats
Their poems. We are all separated.
Your abandoned bivouac should be called
Something like the Orchid Pavilion.

BRIAN LYNCH

The Tea Ceremony

Making tea in the morning
You love, or observe,
The exact ritual.
I'm lying warm in your bed
And you're barefoot in the kitchen.
(When both are habitual,
Love and observe are the same.)

One slice of toast with marmalade.
One cup of tea. One cigarette.
Me getting dressed.
You in your old kimono.

I kiss you lightly and go out.
Sometimes I even come back for more.

But now, I think,
That's where the trouble started:
The pleasure corrupted the joy
As super added spoils the man,
I got the habit of my habit,
Though I don't blame myself.
Oh no, I blame the Mitsuoko,
Your perfume, on my clothes,
It was too much for me,
I had to have it.

DEREK MAHON

The Snow Party

for Louis Asekoff

Bashō, coming
To the city of Nagoya,
Is asked to a snow party.

There is a tinkling of china
And tea into china;
There are introductions.

Then everyone
Crowds to the window
To watch the falling snow.

Snow is falling on Nagoya
And farther south
On the tiles of Kyōto;

Eastward, beyond Irago,
It is falling
Like leaves on the cold sea.

Elsewhere they are burning
Witches and heretics
In the boiling squares,

Thousands have died since dawn
In the service
Of barbarous kings;

But there is silence
In the houses of Nagoya
And the hills of Ise.

Bashō in Kinsale

Samurai cries from
Enthusiasts in the gym
As I wander home.

Dithery rain-lines;
Crows glisten in the branches
Of listening pines.

Gulls in the clear air,
Hawthorn snow in the hedges;
Soon you will be here.

March, evening shadow
On pine and quiet dockyard
Here in Hokkaido.

Clouds obscure the night
Giving our eyes a rest from
The intense moonlight.

Rough sea after dark;
Blazing over the harbour
The fierce zodiac.

A heron voice harsh
Above us after midnight
Like a lightning-flash.

Walking each evening
At a slower pace, we hear
The dark river sing.

A morning of mist;
No light-source but a hidden
Sun burns in the east.

A cove, flies and fleas,
Wrack magic in salt sea-air
And the faintest breeze.

These old childish things,
Big blisters at the shoreline,
Are my water wings.

Blown sand and no talk,
Even the most northern road
An easier walk.

Desert island books:
Homer and Rachel Carson,
Durable hardbacks.

Sketch of a sail race,
The work of many summers:
A few lines in space.

AIDAN CARL MATHEWS

Bashō's Rejected Jottings

for Bill Brown

1. *How to Read Them*
You could do worse
Than begin like children
By smelling the pages.

2. *Winter*
Nothing at all
In the absence
Of so much snow.

3. *Sleep*
My soiled workclothes
Turning slowly
In the cold cycle.

4. *Libraries*
Culture, calm, and so forth.
I could go on.

Two desks down,
She's kicked off her shoes.

5. *Bashō Makes his Move*
When she looks up,
Her head breaks
Water like silence.

6. *Enigma*
All of her that I know
Is a name half-hidden
On a window envelope.

7. *Tête-à-tête*
Small talk through the small hours.
The fire's
Daffodils are cupped asters.

8. *Spring*
Grass through the pavestones
The short hairs
Curling from her cut-offs.

9. *Bashō Accused*
The committee has said
I am a subjectivist,

Or some other big word
Like *respiratory system*.

10. *Midnight*
Please, I say ...
The river
Glistening like wheat.

11. *Courtship*
Her feet were cold all night.
Another
Figure of speech sent packing.

12. *Her Waste-bin*
Eight fingernails.
The other kept
For plucking strings.

13. *Bashō Observes her Sewing*
So delicately
She might be picking
Grit from my eyelid.

14. *Submission*
She paints her nails,
Holding them up to dry.

Her frock lifts at the knee.
Don't. I surrender.

15. *Lights-out*
I'm in luck—
Her nightdress still

Folded up
In the pink rabbit.

16. *Hollows*
Her left armpit
Chafed from shaving.

I mouthwash
Apricot talcum.

17. *Unfinished Haiku*
Someone rang
At the crucial moment.
Never mind.

18. *Fetish*
He brings her small onions
Only to watch
Her eyeshadow spoil.

19. *Acts of Love*
In the morning,
My hands smell
Of beaches after storms.

20. *Codes*
I know when you're bleeding.
You wear
Mauve hair-clips and peep-toe shoes.

21. *Bashō in Love is Prolific*
Two haikus
In a month.
Stop rushing.

22. *Love Compared to Trees*
Roots, we said, *roots,*
Never hearing
The branches creaking like boats.

23. *Endpiece*
Her parting thought
On the begged-for aerogram:
Wear vests if you're out late.

24. *Linguaphone*
Sound stuff.
The first lesson always
On saying goodbye.

25. *She Phones for the First Time*
Bashō, she pleads,
This is all
In your imagination.

26. *Bashō's Retort*
That hair in the futon,
Dark at its root,

From one of two places
Made it here.

27. *Solitude on a Leap Day*
I reach it like a last sand-dune,
Too far off for the others,
One bird among no tar at all.

28. *Defrosting*
The ice-tray
Making *splat* sounds.

Lamb's blood
From which Sunday?

29. *Later Still*
Her soaked hairs
Tugged
From the blocked sink-hole.

30. *Bashō Revises his Poem on Time*
Watch your step.
Two berries, there,
Near the tortoise shit.

31. *Freeze-up*
Light the third bar,
Then climb back in

To watch her pet-name
Melting on the window.

32. *Bad Autumn*
Yet the tomatoes
Have pulled through
In the thickened plot.

33. *Love Notes in the Mail*
My letter-box a pigeon-hole
Where a rare bird lights

Among the xeroxed trash
Of third-class mail.

34. *Reconciliation*
When you come back,
Your hands smell
Of walking gloveless.

JOHN McAULIFFE

Japan

The weather is coming down around them and filling up the
 fields
but they are Sunday drivers, stuck in a dead end, with their
 heads
buried all the while in table-sized road maps that approximate
to where they live, in what we'll call the Hall of the Present
 Life,
its walls loud and impermeable as radio and its roof screwed
 shut
so they rarely notice the emissaries of the Hall of the Western
 Paradise
who dwell among them at crossroads, in courtyards and
 country lanes,
who take many guises, whose form is fluid and inconstant,
who will receive the souls of the dying believers,
who on their vests wear the names of those who paid for their
 creation,
who carry in one hand a rope for binding, and in the other
 a knife.

JAMES McCABE

from *Cliara Haiku* I—XXX

III
Roonagh, rust and rope,
Bearded seaweed walls, old chains
Dancing in the swell.

IV
Clew Bay like a school
Of dolphins, with Clare Island
Like a humpbacked whale.

IX
Listen carefully—
You can hear a thousand ghosts
All speaking Gaelic.

XI
With all my heart I
Hear the heartbroken, carefree
Cry of the curlew.

XII
Cliara abbey—
Littered with the dead, the ground
Itself looks like waves.

XXV
The sweeping beam of
The old lighthouse a thing of
The past, a dreamt dream.

XXIX
Clare Island autumn—
The leaves of long vanished trees
Fall in their millions.

THOMAS McCARTHY

Japanese Bell

Who gave that Buddhist bell to the wandering duke?
It's very far from the Zen world to Kildare.
There wasn't much ascetism in a Victorian peer.
In Japan he got more than a look;
he got the full metal, tongue and bell,
a thousand years of thought, before he sailed.

MEDBH McGUCKIAN

The Flower Master

Like foxgloves in the school of the grass moon
We come to terms with shade, with the principle
Of enfolding space. Our scissors in brocade,
We learn the coolness of straight edges, how
To gently stroke the necks of daffodils
And make them throw their heads back to the sun.

We slip the thready stems of violets, delay
The loveliness of the hibiscus dawn with quiet ovals,
Spirals of feverfew like water splashing,
The papery legacies of bluebells. We do
Sea-fans with sea-lavender, moon-arrangements
Roughly for the festival of moon-viewing.

This black container calls for sloes, sweet
Sultan, dainty nipplewort, in honour
Of a special guest, who summoned to the
Tea ceremony, must stoop to our low doorway,
Our fontanelle, the trout's dimpled feet.

The Butterfly Farm

The film of a butterfly ensures that it is dead:
Its silence like the green cocoon of the car-wash,
Its passion for water to uncloud.

In the Japanese tea house they believe
In making the most of the bright nights:
That the front of a leaf is male, the back female.

There are grass stains on their white stockings;
In artificial sun even the sound are disposable;
The mosaic of their wings is spun from blood.

Cyanide in the killing-jar relaxes the Indian moon moth,
The pearl-bordered beauty, the clouded yellow,
The painted lady, the silver-washed blue.

The Bird Calendar

I never thought of them together
So close to other boats,
This creasing at the wrist of a sunburnt
Male arm drawing her hand
In its unfinished sleeve,
With this brown-gold crouching Venus
Shown with her mouth bound
Over a valence of shot greens and mauves.

Each time I came back crushed
By the swept-back curtain, the gold
Thread in her silk hair-bag
That once had a narrower fall,
The graceful cascade of sheets
From a notte, a night-scene,
Marked by his opalescent touch,
The elegant pink slipper he has signed.

Only years separate them within,
Like the faraway red on a childbirth tray,
An April setting in the winter of words,
The abandoned plough which signals autumn.
I listen to the streets breathe a second,
Hundreds of miles of new streets
Breathing a saffron scent of make-believe
Countryside and warmer buildings,

And call it his Japan, his view of the road,
A more untouched road piercing the forest,
Reconciled to the river as a cushion
For the bridge, the leap of its comforting
Arches: call this slim luxurious window
The garden as a happy refuge
Or a site for danger, this squarish leaf
A sharply defined, glistening tree
By the principle of glittering
And the assumption of enough blue
To give the feel of air to the blue
Enflowered cathedral rougher than the russet
Of a poor twisted Christ of the twelfth century—
Simplified, in the moist outdoor imitation,
Evidence of a sky, a simple blue sky,
At the lighted edge of the wall.

PETER McMILLAN

Broken Ink Landscape

In Japan
the broken ink
landscape
is a meditation
on being and
non-being,
on what hovers
for a moment
in the landscape
and what lasts
a very long time.

Being is captured
as it *appears*,
as if that is the way
it really is.
Light and space
are mostly un-painted
or done in the palest wash.
Tiny sharp figures,
a hut,
a boat,
a flock
of over-flying birds
bearing immanence
on their wings
bring scale,
distance,
grace.

The ink landscape
is the art of non-
painting.
Blank space
can evoke all.
One can drown in
Sesshu's great expanse
of unpainted water
and Mu-chi'i's sky
reaches all the way
to heaven.

The words
—*Gossamer*
—*Cloud light*
—*Heron blue*
describe
these works of art.
Or one can invent
new words
not come
into language yet.

The ink landscape
is born of stillness.
But the sad lament
of the over-flying birds
pierces the paper,
murmuring waves
dampen the edges,
and soft breezes
of evening
blot the distinction
between mountain,
mist, lake and cloud.

Night thickens.
The birds fly off
and the scene of
a lone fisherman
on a silver lake
in soft washes
bold strokes of ink
and empty space
re-creates itself.

The momentary passes.
The lasting re-appears
as another immanence.
In the plaintive cry
of a snipe
—a tiny curved V—
rising slowly
from the reeds at dusk,
or a three-day old
sliver of moon,
a delicate arc
of white left blank,
or in the fisherman's bait
at the end of the line
cast out by the artist
into the fugitive heart of being

from **Hyakunin Isshu**

Kakinomoto no Hitomaro (?— ca. 707)

The
long
tail
of
the
copper
pheasant
trails–
drags
on
and
on
like
this
long
night
in
the
lonely
mountains
where
like
that
bird
I
too
must
sleep
without
my
love.

TED McNULTY

Dreaming in Japanese

The spider competing for the prize
in geometry has made a net
of white lines in rhomboid modes
As judge I remove my shoes
to waver like a sailor
on rigging between great spars
as I walk across the spider's web
inch along thick silken ropes
held in the curl of my toes
while sudden at the edge of my eye
a moving pillar of a shape
like the mast of the tallest ship
to set sail from Japan.

PAULA MEEHAN

The First Day of Winter

My head in the clouds
in the bowl of Akiko's
mother's white miso.

DOROTHY MOLLOY

Four Haikus

Sunlight in gutter,
butterbright, apricot, peach,
October, leaf-thief.

~

In the tall windows
of their eyes, cats crouch, under
pelmets of warm fur.

~

Cats knead on my knees,
pumping paws, piercing claws, I
bleed. Oh, but the purrs.

~

Purple hearts sprouting
unseen in the forests of
winter broccoli.

SINÉAD MORRISSEY

Goldfish

The black fish under the bridge was so long I mistook it
for a goldfish in a Japanese garden the kind the philosophers
wanted about them so much gold underwater to tell them what waited
in another element like breathing water they wanted to go
to the place where closing eyes is to see

I understood the day I closed my eyes in Gifu City I saw Japan
for the first time saw what I had seen the gate to the Nangu
Shrine by the Shinkansen stood straddled before my head and I
held out my hands to touch it and felt changed air it wasn't
there but I walked into it continually and over the gardens full
of pumpkin seeds in the ground and wild red flowers over them
                                                                           they told me

they brought autumn and they were about my head also in Gifu
                                                      City all pearled
in mist and happy as Japanese brides. I saw the JR crates on the night
trains that passed through stations and seemed endless and running
on purpose on time's heels on sheer will to cross Honshu one end
to the other money's own messenger fire down the line. And when
                                                you talked me through

Gifu one end to the other eyes closed I saw what I would never
have seen sighted a transvestite taxi driver set apart on the street
a lost person flowers by the pavement pavements for the blind I saw
music as pulled elastic bands drums as the footprints of exacting gods

I mistook the black fish for an oriental goldfish the flash of gold
on its belly meant it carried its message for the element below it
always one storey down Zen masters attaining one storey down and I,
falling into you, story by story, coming to rest in the place where
closing eyes is to see

Night Drive in Four Metaphors

I want the woman driving I don't know never to stop
driving us by rice fields on the narrowest roads
that are straight as the line through the kanji for 'centre'—
The eye of an animal skewered and shown on its side.

The smoke from the factories lights up tonight as a gate to a fallen-
down moon.
A moon on its back under the shadow of its circle is a unique moon.
It means home is under the weight of a stone and that brightness can
come from under a shadow—
The whole weight of a cold ball breathing on it and look how it smiles.

The flats for Brazilian factory workers have shirts hung out on
balconies to dry.
The shirts are coloured by game shows and adverts for shampoo.
Full as scarecrows, lines across and lines down of them—
The buildings are ships on a wind sea trying to sail.

And you beside me with your hair overgrown watching the other
side of the world.
Imagine how the stars are split between my window and yours!
The join is unimaginable from under the roof of the car—
Two worlds split open to each other, stars spilling from each.

Between Here and There

No one seems sure of the reason why aprons
are tied to the necks of stone babies in temples.
The priest says 'honour'.
The guide to Kyoto City mentions 'cold
on their journey away from us to the heaven for children'.
I look at them squatting in Buddha-reflection,
wrapped up to the throat in teddy bears and trains.

~

There's a graveyard for miscarriages under Ikeda Mountain
as stark as a bone field. No flowers, tangerines, sake or aprons
but a basin of stone bodies in two parts: square body, round head.
Like oriental soldiers contained by a wall, they would go walking—
spill over with all of the energy for life that fell out of them too soon.
Except that even in stone some bodies have opened—
loose balls in the basin where heads have rolled.

~

Inside the biggest wooden building in the world
sits Japan's greatest Buddha. One hand raised as a stop sign to evil.
The other is flat, flat with comfort and promise, flat enough
for all of us to nuzzle his thumb. His lily flower opened.
His crossing was a falling into light.
Fall with me, he says, *and you'll be raised to the heights
of the roof of the biggest wooden building in the world.*

~

When Nagasawa visits the house of the dead
he leaves at the door his camera and tripod
his champion karaoke voice his miracle foot massage
his classroom dynamics his rockhard atheism
and slips onto the tatami of the prayer room
as the man who can chant any you-name-it soul
between here and Ogaki to paradise.

Nagasawa in Training

Thirty years, say,
since you left your father's temple
for your father's mother temple in Kyoto.

Eight weeks in training. Prayers for the dead
at four in the morning and a lantern over the stairway.
It lit up your face in papery gloom.

From six until eight
you washed four hundred year-old wooden platforms
stopped dead over latticed bamboo

while the sun came over the TV tower
and the colour of the day
began in earnest to upset you.

Lovers lit up in the long grass!
Three hundred and sixty degrees of crashed renegades
all getting up, getting rid of the dew.

You had two broken hearts, a wife
from your father's books awaiting you
and damage, a sense of it, leaking into you.

Before the years came with their appointments, their daughters,
a neighbourhood to pray for and a cancer constituency,
sex was as stark to you

as the room of nothing you were building in your head.
There was nothing to diffuse the light of that morning.
Nothing but moaning and nothing left of you.

To Encourage the Study of Kanji

I've been inside these letters it seems for years, I've drawn them
on paper, palms, steamed mirrors and the side of my face
in my sleep, I've waded in sliced lines and crossed boxes.

They stay, stars in the new-moon sky,
as dead as the names of untraceable constellations.
Intricate, aloof, lonely, abstracted,

some other mind made them and still since then
they've shrunk to a hint at a fairytale. Say I thread beads.
Say I remember a sky of walking pictures.

PAUL MULDOON

The Narrow Road to the Deep North

A Japanese soldier
Has just stumbled out of the forest.
The war has been over
These thirty years, and he has lost

All but his ceremonial sword.
We offer him an American cigarette.
He takes it without a word.
For all this comes too late. Too late

To break the sword across his knee,
To be right or wrong.
He means to go back to his old farm

And till the land. Though never to deny
The stone its sling,
The blade of grass its one good arm.

Sushi

'Why do we waste so much time in arguing?'
We were sitting at the sushi-bar
drinking *Kirin* beer
and watching the Master chef
fastidiously shave

salmon, tuna and yellowtail
while a slightly more volatile
apprentice
fanned the rice,
every grain of which was magnetized
in one direction—east.
Then came translucent strips
of octopus,
squid and conger,
pickled ginger
and pale-green horseradish . . .
'It's as if you've some kind of death-wish.
You won't even talk . . .'
On the sidewalk
a woman in a leotard
with a real leopard
in tow.
For an instant I saw beyond the roe
of sea-urchins,
the erogenous
zones of shad and sea-bream;
I saw, when the steam
cleared, how this apprentice
had scrimshandered a rose's
exquisite petals
not from some precious metal
or wood or stone
('I might just as well be eating alone.')
but the tail-end of a carrot:
how when he submitted this work of art
to the Master—
Is it not the height of arrogance
to propose that God's no more arcane
than the smack of oregano,

orgone,
the inner organs
of beasts and fowls, the mines of Arigna,
the poems of Louis Aragon?—
it might have been alabaster
or jade
the Master so gravely weighed
from hand to hand
with the look of a man unlikely to confound
Duns Scotus, say, with Scotus Eriugena.

The Point

Not Sato's sword, not Sato's "consecrated blade"
that for all its years in the oubliette
of Thoor Ballylee is unsullied, keen,
lapped yet in the lap of a geisha's gown.

Not the dagger that Hiroo Onoda
would use again and again to undo
the frou-frous, the fripperies, the Fallopian
tubes of a dead cow in the Philippines.

What everything in me wants to articulate
is this little bit of a scar that dates
from the time O'Clery, my schoolroom foe,

rammed his pencil into my exposed *thigh*
(not, as the chronicles have it, my calf)
with such force that the point was broken off.

Nightingales

I

"In great contrast to the nightingale's pre-eminent voice
is the inconspicuous coloration of its plumage,"
as Alfred Newton so winningly puts it

in his *Dictionary of Birds*. I fell in love with a host face
that showed not the slightest blemish.
They tell me her makeup was powdered nightingale shit.

II

They tell me the Japanese nightingale's not a nightingale
but a Persian bulbul. Needless to say, it's the male bird
that's noted for opening the floodgates
and pouring out its soul, particularly during nesting season.

III

Now they tell me a network of wedges and widgets and wooden nails
has Nijojo Castle's floorboards
twitter "like nightingales." This twittering warned the shogunate
of unwelcome guests. Wide boys. Would-be assassins.

from *Hopewell Haiku*

I

The door of the shed
open-shuts with the clangor
of red against red.

III

From whin-bright Cave Hill
a blackbird might... *will* give thanks
with his whin-bright bill.

VIII

Snow up to my shanks.
I glance back. The path I've hacked
is a white turf bank.

XV

The changeless penknife.
The board. The heavy trestles.
The changeless penknife.

XVII

The finer the cloth
in your obi, or waist piece,
the finer the moth.

XXV

A hammock at dusk.
I scrimshaw a narwhal hunt
on a narwhal tusk.

XXVII

The yard's three lonesome
pines are hung with such tokens.
A play by Zeami.

XXVIII

Good Friday. At three,
a swarm of bees sets its heart
on an apple tree.

XXXII

We buy flour, bacon
and beans with pollen we pan
here in the Yukon.

XXXVII

The bold Pangur Ban
draws and quarters a wood thrush
by the garbage can.

XLI

Jean paints one toenail.
In a fork of the white ash,
quick, a cardinal.

L

Now I must take stock.
The ax I swaggered and swung's
split the chopping block.

LIV

An airplane, alas,
is more likely than thunder
to trouble your glass.

LVII

While from the thistles
that attend our middle age
a goldfinch whistles.

LIX

Wonder of wonders.
The plow that stood in the hay's
itself plowed under.

LXI

Bivouac. Billet.
The moon a waning of lard
on a hot skillet.

LXVI

Two trees in the yard
bring neither shade nor shelter
but rain, twice as hard.

LXVII

A bullfrog sumo
stares into his bowl of wine.
Those years in Suma.

LXXV

I've upset the pail
in which my daughter had kept
her five—"No, *six*"—snails.

LXXVII

Is that body bag
Cuchulainn's or Ferdia's?
Let's check the dog tag.

LXXVIII

Fresh snow on the roof
of a car that passed me by.
The print of one hoof.

LXXIX

Though the cankered peach
is felled, the bird's nest it held
is still out of reach.

LXXX

The stag I sideswiped.
I watched a last tear run down
his tear duct. I wept.

LXXXVII

Not a golden carp
but a dog turd under ice.
Not a golden carp.

XC

The maple's great cask
that once held so much in store
now yields a hip flask.

GERRY MURPHY

The Ferbane Haiku

Long live nothingness
beyond this puny heart-song
this wretched wheezing.

Bite your whining tongue
the loveliest woman here
is looking at you.

Cancel the doctor
this naked conversation
is healing enough.

Haiku for Norman McCaig

The bittern's lament
recalling the giddy soul
to its loneliness.

Ballynoe Haiku

My kisses like bees
in your honey-coloured hair
sweetly mistaken.

Your kisses like rain
on the forgotten desert
of my abdomen.

NUALA NÍ DHOMHNAILL

Sneachta

Níor cheol éan,
níor labhair damh,
níor bhéic tonn,
níor lig rón sceamh.

Snow

No bird sang
no stag spoke
no seal roared
no wave broke

JULIE O'CALLAGHAN

after Sei Shonagon

Time

Only a moment ago
he lay beside me
saying silly poetic things.
The mat is still warm,
incense from his robe
haunts the air.

Lady Hyobu

as you all know
is a great friend of mine.
But we don't get on
when it comes to calligraphy.
I was practising my characters
in her room last week
when she said to me,
'Would you mind
not using that brush?'
I never say things like that
if she uses my best brush
or keeps asking what's
inside my writing box
or lets the bristles

soak forever in ink
so they're ruined.
Another thing—
it's very annoying
when I'm sitting there
trying to work on a poem
and she gives me a dirty look
and orders me out of her light.

A View of Mount Fuji

for Patrick Scott

When Emperor Ichijo
asked me what I wanted
as a parting gift
I answered Mount Fuji.

Towards the end
of the Third Month
a Court Chamberlain
led me to new quarters.

I lit a charcoal fire,
arranged my combs and fans
the way I like them
and took in my surroundings.

The lattice was decorated
with patterns of gold leaf
and as I raised the blind
Mount Fuji waited in the distance.

Here I give you Fuji-san
dressed in imperial robes
so that you will not forget me.
He was mine.

Two Lines

The gentlemen of the Sixth Rank
must be easily pleased.
They have been over-praising
two lines I scribbled
with an old piece of charcoal
late at night.
It was something about
visiting a grass-thatched hut
and who would bother
with such a lowly place.
But now I hear
how the Court Nobles
have copied it onto their fans!
His Excellency Tadanobu
even came and pounded
on my half-shutters
looking like the hero
from a romance.
The sleeves from his grape jacket
draped over my screen
are the best reward.

21st Century Pillow Book

In Traffic

Three things which
should never be seen
in traffic:
phone at ear
obscene finger gesture
speeding teenager

Office

Three conundrums:
collection for person you can't stand
overhearing colleagues gossip about you
staying awake during boring meeting

Fashion Trends

Yes yes—I realise I am not a young person
so call me an old biddy if you want
but this wearing of tight little tops
with midriffs on view—idiotic.
Blubber is not real gorgeous.
And teaming that with low tight jeans
only makes it worse.
Even if the blub is minimal
the waistbands are so snug
that any flesh at all bunches up
and hangs over
in almost every case.

We have no wish to see this.
When future generations
see photos of you,
you will thank me
for this advice.

Plastic Surgery

No one wants to get old anymore.
You might see a woman
with a dewy complexion
not a wrinkle or line or sag
and envy her beauty.
Then several days later
you hear she has had a face lift.
How confusing.

Skyscrapers

Nothing can be more deeply moving
than standing on the roof
of a 30-storey building
in the dark
beside a shimmering pool
of turquoise water
and gazing down at the city
in all directions.
A balmy summer night.
Stars overhead.
Lights from other buildings
quiet in the distance.
Happiness.
Sadness.

Children

Why do parents these days
pamper and spoil their offspring?
I will never understand it.
Gucci baby booties, Dior romper suits,
tiny tots math classes and personal trainers
and mini computer programs.
A four year old, being driven to
his Mozart appreciation class,
warns his mother
to be sure to pick him up on time.
He doesn't want to miss
his favourite cartoon.
Has the world gone crazy?

Things that Fall from the Sky

dying embers from fireworks
box kites on a still day
faulty satellites
badly serviced airplanes
acid rain
ducks shot in the chest
flying saucers

Things without Merit

reality TV shows
nuclear waste
OTT bling
Hollywood actors giving interviews
pop stars giving interviews
frozen supermarket meals

Things that Should be Large

Pay checks. Valentine cards. Pretzels.
It is very important
for a special birthday party
to be large—
otherwise people will think
you are a loser.
That goes for engagement rings
and bank balances and dogs.
I recommend a Great Dane.
Large horses, it's true,
are the only ones
worth having.

Pleasing Things

Don't you just love it
when the best parking place is empty?
And you have an EU passport
and are waved through
when all the other jetlagged Americans
have to get in a long line
—now THAT is pleasing.
You are searching for a particular
jar of spaghetti sauce
and after rearranging a few others
you see one jar left
at the back of the shelf.
But the most pleasing thing
is coming across
completely by accident
something you know will
make the perfect gift
for someone you love.

Calligraphy

I

Reading a Letter

She has waited
beside her charcoal fire for days
and now receives an answer.

It is a small twig
with two buds
and full pear blossom,

wrapped in the palest
lavender rice paper.
She smiles; smells the blossom.

II

A Meeting

They lie together
all night whispering
and touching cheeks.
The shutters are open
that face the garden;
they dread the first
bird calls that start
the morning off.

III

A Heian Lady

The silk she wears
reflects the season.
In daylight she is shy,
hides behind a painted screen.
At night she hates a mosquito

to flutter its wings near her face.
She writes a book kept in a pillow.
It says, "It is getting so dark
I can scarcely go on writing;
and my brush is all worn out."

IV

Reincarnation

I have no willow-green robe now
of Chinese damask.
No layers of unlined robes

in peach-colored silk.
No gown of Chinese gauze
with blue prints over white.

Where are my jacket of light violet
lined with scarlet
and my plum-red skirt?

JOHN O'DONNELL

The Wave

> *in memory of those who perished in the Fastnet Yacht Race, 1979*

Grizzled mainsail trimmer off a Yankee clipper
the only one to call it, cloudless August morning
in the shore-side caff. 'Something big

out there in the Atlantic,' southern drawl amid
Sweet Afton, waft of last night's beer, bitching
about skippers over eggs and bacon. Tinkling

masts. The gleam and spank of sail, yachts prancing
in the harbour, courses plotted for The Rock. No runic
satellite, no merry weather-man could then foretell

the mangled spars. The drifting empty hulls.
The sodden bodies hauled aboard by trawlers;
the others, never found, lists taped up in windows

near the greasy spoon where that old salt had seen
what Hokusai saw, beyond the geishas and the fishmarkets
of Edo, his own floating world as he leaned over

a wood-block carved from cherry to make his picture
of the wave off Kanagawa: out of nowhere, a rumble
in the ocean, foam-flecked surge gathering in the arc

of its own rage into a roar of water, brute beauty
trembling above the wooden sampans, the cowering men.
Poised. Ready to sweep everything away.

MARY O'DONNELL

10 Haikus on Love and Death

1.
The man is winter.
His body is a warm cave.
Feel the low fires burn.

2.
Fingers in the soil.
The silent knowledge of roots.
From darkness to light.

3.
They speak of rising.
From what can we rise but death?
Now for the living.

4.
Dog of the spring night,
A frieze of leaves in moonlight,
Frost glitters on fields.

5.
My love's bright flower.
His leaves in a sheen of dew.
His passionate root!

6.
The girls swim like fish.
Hither in the deft ocean.
Minnows seeking warmth.

7.
And if I die now,
Will what is done be enough?
Winter is my judge.

8.
Foxgloves at twilight,
Dipping with purple secrets,
Mauve sheaths drip pollen.

9.
Woman in August.
Her body is a forest.
Here there is welcome.

10.
The red lips of June,
Shirts of sun, ribbons of moon,
How radiant is love!

DESMOND O'GRADY

from *Summer Harvest Renga*

written with Matthew Geden

July is every farmer's
month to reap and bind
what he sowed in spring

    the sun in her hair
    she walks the shore

this dolphin surfaces and dives
in his neighbour's bay
to undulate her wavelets

    ripples in the river ride
    all summer is movement

if on the other hand she's earthy
make hay while the sun shines
to feed all natural appetites

    flowers fill the hedgerows
    with colourful lust for life

nature in summer bloom
surrounds my walk by the river
watch the fish dance underwater

    following your footsteps
    tap out the seasonal beat

rise the croaked chorus of crows
from the church graves
the palaver of pigeons from ruins

    sibilant sweep of the seashore
    shingle shudders in sunshine

here the river flows out
into the ocean under
the setting sun

    at twilight slowness is all
    time to think

memories blink from their distances
until cloud and night
covers with darkness

    somewhere a door shuts
    the harvest is done

TOM O'MALLEY

from Seasonal Haiku

Spring

Another rite of spring—
as clocks move forward one hour
we take the fast lane.

> I clear a patch
> for seeds and seedlings—the weeds
> have their own agenda.

Beamed to chancel wall—
stained glass negatives of saints:
medieval slides.

Summer

Close up—these seagulls
that follow our boat; no need
for binoculars.

> Lovers at airport
> part reluctantly—velcro
> slowly separates.

Dead roadside fox—gone
his mystery, ghostly sightings;
we turn away.

Autumn

Autumn mist—its grey
string-beads betray the spider's
crafty hammocks.

      Stiff from the iron
      your cool white bed linen
      —faint scent of metal.

Carpet fawns and browns
blent with crisp birch leaves, blown in
—my autumn hallway.

Winter

The air warm again—
children's snow sculptures deflate
in green/white gardens.

      A cold season's breath
      from my freezer's open door
      —winter's kept on ice.

Amplified by frost—
from Ballykine wood at dusk
snarls of a chainsaw.

CAITRÍONA O'REILLY

Netsuke

I walk on thin soles
this dense season.

No wind lifts the leaves,
the thickened stream

shakes no reeds.
I spread my fan,

hide half my wan
face, pale with lead,

pale with the shit
of nightingales.

The marks they limn
on my nape

might have been
knife marks,

stark when I blushed
at his figurines:

women and men coiled
round each other

like worms,
a tongue-cut sparrow,

a nest of rats.
They keep his objects

from sliding down
that long silk cord

he hangs beside
his genitals, and being

lost. When I draw
his blade across my

arm it resembles
water dripping over

a stone lip
in the stone garden,

runny wax
from a candle,

the new moon's
incised smile.

FRANK ORSMBY

Six Haiku

The field full of snow
so much a field full of snow
it needs a blackbird

Hares on the grass patch
between the runways. Ears flat.
Ready for take-off.

Sensing a haiku
opportunity—those two
blackbirds, right on cue!

On the yard wall,
suddenly, a hooded crow.
Hard bastard. You can tell.

How relaxed she is,
that stray heifer,
shitting her way through the graveyard.

Missing the fish's jump,
we have to make do
with the splash and its ripples.

CATHAL Ó SEARCAIGH

Duine Corr

    i gcead do Nebojsa Vasovic

Oíche Shathairn agus mé ag baint sú
as mo chuideachta féin, mar is gnáth,
anseo cois tineadh i Mín á Leá—
is breá liom an t-uaigneas seo,
(cé acu i dtrátha nó in antráth)
a bheir cothú don chiúnas.

Ach cha cheadaítear domh
a bheith liom féin ar feadh i bhfad.
Scairteann cairde orm ar ball
a rá go bhfuil siad ar bís
le gníomh a dhéanamh láithreach.
Tá siad ag féachaint ar an teilifís:
cráite ag an ár agus an mharfach
atá ag gabháil ar aghaidh, thall,
i mBosnia agus i Serbia.

Chan fhuil barúil ar bith agam, faraor,
fá Bhosnia ná fá Serbia;
cé atá ciontach nó cé atá saor
nó cé hiad na treibheanna
atá ag troid is ag treascairt a chéile sa tír.
Ach le bheith fíor agus i ndáiríre
dá mbeadh an t-eolas seo agam go beacht
cha bheadh an t-am nó an taithí

nó rud is tábhachtaí, an neart
ionam, le haon chuid den mheascán mearaí seo
a réiteach is a chur ina cheart.

Níl aon ní is mó a theastaíonn uaim
ná fad saoil le suí anseo liom féin
i bhfad ó bhearna an bhaoil,
cois tineadh i Mín á Leá
ag léamh is ag ól tae
is ag machnamh go teacht an lae
ar dhuanaire de dhánta Zen
ón tSeapáin is ón tSín.

Nuair a thiocfas cogadh chun cinn
sa tSeapáin nó sa tSín
lá is faide anonn
beidh mé anseo liom féin
mar is gnách
cois tineadh i Mín á Leá.
Dhéanfaidh mé cupán tae
agus diadh ar ndiaidh
léifidh mé le fonn
bailiúchán de dhánta grá
ó Bhosnia is ó Serbia.

Odd Man Out

after Nebojsa Vasovic

Saturday night, lapping up
my own company as usual,

here by the fire in Mín á Leá,
I really enjoy the solitude
(hail, rain or shine);
it adds to the calmness.

But I'm not allowed
to be on my own for long.
Friends call me in no time
to tell me they are dying
to do something right away.
They're watching tv: tormented
by the murder and slaughter
going on over there
in Bosnia and Serbia.

I haven't a clue, I'm afraid,
about Bosnia or Serbia;
who's to blame and who's not
or who the tribes are,
clubbing each other into the ground.
But really and truly,
if I knew this information inside out
I wouldn't have the time, know-how,
or what's even more important, the power
to solve or put right any of this madness.

All I want is to spend
my life sitting here on my own,
staying the hell-out-of-it
by the hearth in Mín á Leá,
reading, drinking tea
and musing till dawn
on a book of Zen poems
from Japan and China.

And when war comes about
in Japan or China
further down the line,
I'll be here on my own
same as usual,
by the hearth in Mín á Leá.
I'll make a cup of tea
and fervently read,
one by one,
a collection of love poems
from Bosnia and Serbia.

Translated by Frank Sewell

Pilleadh an Deoraí

Teach tréigthe roimhe anocht.
Ar an tairseach, faoi lom na gealaí, nocht,
scáile an tseanchrainn a chuir sé blianta ó shin.

Exile's Return

He's back tonight to a deserted house.
On the doorstep, under a brilliant moon, a stark
shadow: the tree he planted years ago is an old tree.

Translated by Seamus Heaney

MICHEAL O'SIADHAIL

Tsunami 津波

   1
An unheard inner molten command
And the earth's maw begins to retch
Cracking the floor of the Indian Ocean.

Tsu: water and a brush in hand
To sign a sweep of sea, a stretch
Of deep for safe crossing, a haven.

Nami: liquid and a flaying hand
To symbolise a wave, as if to sketch
An ocean peeling off its skin.

Together a billowing towards land,
A tidal wave gathering its fetch
To deliver a long roll of misfortune.

   2
Their flight visceral
And inborn as before it begins
An original
People still read the signs.

Nature's bonds
Broken by stilted inn
Or shrimp ponds
No mangroves hold the line.

Safer at sea:
In shallows the swells heighten,
Irony
Of a harbour now danger's haven.

Earthlings our toss
And turn frail in the sweep
Of a cosmos,
Humble riders on a moody spaceship,

A trembling globe.
Some hundred and eighty thousand.
Like Job
We cry out what is our end?

   3
That all would have died sometime.
Any death as much a riddle as thousands.
So many together, unripe, in their prime?

Whole kindred with no one to claim
Their hurried dead or still to remember
A vanished face or a cried name.

Never to be called 'old man' *Bapak!*
Days into days stretch into weeks
And tides sweep over the crack

As an orphan blows her toy trumpet
Sumatra's grievers show signs of return
Setting out fruits at a morning market.

Durian, papaya, lime and mangostan.
Our earth is spinning across its seasons.
Fishermen cling to the skin of an ocean.

EOGHAN Ó TUAIRISC

Three sections from 'Aifreann na Marbh'

Fuair Bás ag Hiroshima
Dé Luain, 6ú Lúnasa, 1945

"*Transumanar significar per verba*
non si poria; però l'esemplo basti
a cui esperïenza Grazia serba"
—*Dante, Paradiso, I, 70-72*

1. *Introitus*

Músclaíonn an mhaidin ár míshuaimhneas síoraí.
Breathnaím trí phána gloine
Clogthithe na hÁdhamhchlainne
Ár gcuid slinn, ár gCré, ár gcúirteanna
Ar snámh san fhionnuaire.
Nochtann as an rosamh chugam
An ghlanchathair mhaighdeanúil
Ag fearadh a haiséirí:
Músclaíonn an mhaidin ár míshuaimhneas síoraí.

Broinnean an ceatal binnuaigneach i mo chroí
Ar fheiscint dom a háilleachta,
Géagshíneadh a gealsráideanna
Le hais na habhann, na coillte,
Líne na gcnoc pinnsilteach
Á háitiú ina céad riocht—
Mo chailín cathrach fornocht
Ina codladh ag áth na gcliath:
Músclaíonn an mhaidin ár míshuaimhneas síoraí.

Trí mhír as 'Aifreann na Marbh'

> Died in Hiroshima
> Monday, 6th June, 1945
>
> "*Transumanar significar per verba
> non si poria; però l'esemplo basti
> a cui esperïenza Grazia serba*"
> —Dante, *Paradiso*, I, 70-72

1. *Introit*

The morning arouses our unceasing unease.
From behind a pane of glass I look out
At the bell towers of the Adam-clan:
Our slates, our creed, our lawcourts
Floating in the freshness.
Out of the haze
The virginal bright city
Unveils herself for me,
Offering resurrection.
The morning arouses our unceasing unease.

The lonely-sweet pang in my heart
Stirs at the sight of her beauty,
Stretching her limbs, her bright streets,
Beside the river. And the woods
And the line of the trickling hill-peaks
Establish her in her hundred guises,
My girl-city stark naked
Sleeping by the wattle-ford.
The morning arouses our unceasing unease.

Tagann an aisling rinnuaibhreach anoir,
Scaipeann rós is airgead
Trí smúit a calafoirt
Ina lá léaspairte, súnas
Ag éigniú a maighdeanais
Nó go bhfágtar gach creat
Gach simléar, gach seolchrann
Ina chnámh dhubh, ina ghrianghraf
Ag léiriú inmhíniú mo laoi:
Músclaíonn an mhaidin ár míshuaimhneas síoraí.

2. Kyrie

Siú Íosasú, amhaireimí tama-i!*

Déan trócaire orainn atá gan trócaire
Dár n-ainmhian eolaíochta déan trua,
Foilsigh trí shalachar na haimsire
A chruthaíomar dúinn féin, an ghrian nua.
D'aimsíomar an t-úll
D'fhág an tseanghrian faoi smál, *Siú Íosasú.*

Amhaireimí. Orainne ar na sráideanna
Chuireas cos thar chois amach ar maidin Luain
Gan aird againn ar ár gcuid scáileanna
Ag gliúchadh orainn ón ngloine, an dara slua

**Lord Jesus, have mercy on us! (This prayer was heard on the streets of Hiroshima on the morning of the tragedy).*

The dream-vision out of the east, planet-proud,
Comes and scatters roseate-silver light
Among the grime of her harbour;
Comes as sparkling day, blinding,
And violates her virginity
Till each chimney, each beam
And ship's mast
Is reduced to black bone,
To photographic negative,
Bringing out the meaning of my verse:
The morning arouses our unceasing unease.

Translated by Aidan Hayes with Anna Ní Dhomhnaill

2. Kyrie

Siú Íosasú, amhaireimí tama-i!*

Have mercy on us who are without mercy,
Have pity on our lust for science.
Through the grime of the era
That we ourselves created
Show the new sun.
We split the apple
And left the old sun ash-coated. *Siú Íosasú.*

Amhaireimí, mercy on us who step out briskly
On the streets on a Monday morning,
Blind to the company of our bright shadows
Who peer at us from window-glass:

* *"A Thiarna Íosa, déan trócaire orainn!" (Chualathas an phaidir sin ar shráideanna Hiroshima maidin na tragóide).*

Ar choiscéim linn go ciúin
Mílítheach marbh múinte. *Siú Íosasú.*

Siú. Siúlaim. Trí thionóisc na dteangacha
Gluaisim ar aghaidh ag machnamh ar an mbua
A bhaineamar amach, eolas na maitheasa
Agus an oilc i dtoil an té gan stiúir
Ina dhia beag ar siúl—
Amhaireimí. Amhaireimí. Siú Íosasú.

Siúd liom isteach trí áirse ollscoile
Ag snámh ina n-aghaidh, an t-aos óg gealsnua
A bhrúchtann chun solais lena málaí ascaille
Ag trácht ar an spás, an teoragán is nua,
An fhinnbheannach, an mhongrua
Is a dtálchuid faoi chuing na matamaitice. *Siú.*

Fanann a gcumhracht liom ar ghaoth a n-imeachta
Fanann seal nóiméid sa phasáiste cúng
Niamhracht agus naí-gháire na n-aoiseanna
A cnuasaíodh i bhfriotal binn nach buan,
D'éalaigh na nimfeacha uainn
Ach maireann mil a nginiúna faoin áirse againn. *Siú.*

Dearcaim arís trí shúile freacnairce
An chloch dhiúltach, an chearnóg mhanachúil,
Suaimhneas an chlabhstair ar a chearchall aislinge
Nach músclaítear ag clogdhán ná ag an uaill
Bhalbh phianstairiúil
I gcroílár an róis crochta chois balla. *Siú.*

Luaitear na dátaí, ainmneacha ailtirí,
Comhrá cneasta cinnte coillte acadúil,

A second crowd of walkers
Quietly walking in step with our step,
Pale. Dead. Tamed. *Siú Íosasú.*

Siú. I walk. Through the accident of languages
I move on, reflecting on our triumph—
The knowledge of good and evil
Under the control of the uncontrolled one
Like a little god in its progress.
Amhaireimí. Amhaireimí. Siú Íosasú.

In through a university archway,
Breasting the stream of bright young faces,
Bags on shoulders, pushing toward the light,
Discussing space, the latest theorem—
The blonde heads and the red—
Their contribution under mathematics' yoke. *Siú.*

Their freshness stays in the draught their passing makes:
Pausing a moment in the narrow passageway,
The shine and young laughter of the ages
That was stored in fragile sweet speech.
The nymphs stole away from us,
But the honey of their begetting stays
Under this arch of ours. *Siú.*

Through contemporary eyes I look again
At the stubborn stone, the monastic square,
The quiet of the cloister, the circle of its dream-vision
That will not be aroused by the bell,
Nor the mute pain-filled howl of history
That's deep in the heart of the rose that hangs by the wall. *Siú.*

Dates are cited, the names of architects,
The confident discourse of mild-mannered gelded academics.

Ní ligtear le fios i bhfocal paiseanta
Ainm an ailtire a dhearaigh an bunstua
Ní luaitear lá an Luain
Nó go labhraíonn an gairbhéal gáirsiúil faoinár sála. *Siú.*

Tagann tollbhlosc ón bhfaiche imeartha
Ag méadú an chiúnais is ag cur in iúl
Dhíomhaointeas an dísirt ina bhfuilimid
Faoi aghaidheanna fidil leanbaí ag súil
Nach dtitfidh an tromchúis
Orainne, cé go screadann na rósanna as croí a gcumhrachta. *Siú.*

Fiosraím an fál in uaigneas leabharlainne,
An litir ársa is an dobharchú
Ag breith ar an iasc i gcoidéacs Cheannannais
Idir an crot is a chéasadh, an dá rún,
Ag ceangal an chlabhsúir
San ainm seang a mharaigh mé. *Siú Íosasú.*

Siú. Siúl. Siúlaim. Siúlaimid
Trí réimniú briathar, faí mharfach, ar aghaidh
Ó Luan go Luan ag ceapadh suaitheantais
In eibhearchloch na cathrach seo gan aidhm,
Tá an cailín ina haghaidh.
Siú Íosasú, amhaireimí tama-i.

Not conveyed in passionate words,
The name of the architect of the original arch.
The fatal Monday goes unmentioned
Till the bawdy gravel's voice is heard under our heels. *Siú*.

A piercing roar comes from the playing-field,
Deepening the quiet and bringing home
The sterility of the desert where we are,
Behind our childish masks, hoping
The heavy consequences don't fall on us
Even though the roses are screaming from their fragrant core. *Siú*.

In the solitude of the library I seek answers—
The noble lettering and the otter
Seizing the fish in the codex of Kells.
Between the conception and its crucifixion,
The two secrets binding the conclusion of the work,
The emaciated name of the one I killed. *Siú Íosasú*.

Siú. Walk. I am walking. We are walking
Through conjugations of verbs, the fatal whine,
Onward from Monday to Monday inventing emblems
In the granite blocks of this purposeless city:
The girl-woman stands against it.
Siú Íosasú, amhaireimí tama-i.

Translated by Aidan Hayes with Anna Ní Dhomhnaill

3. Graduale

Ná tóg orm a Chríost
Go ndearnas an ghadaíocht
Is foirm do cheatail ghlinn
A dhealbhú dom aisling,

Buairt m'anama nach beag
I mo sheasamh ar chéimeanna
Na cathrach céasta, ceannocht,
Is cúis dom an ghadaíocht.

Sinne na mairbh fuair bás
In Áth Cliath is in antráth
Lá gréine na blasféime
Shéideamar Hiroshima.

Ní Gaeil sinn a thuilleadh de shloinneadh Ír is Éibhir,
Ní hoíche linn an spéirling a fuineadh do bhláth Dhéirdre,
An tráth seo chois Life an loingis i gcríon mo laetha
Is léir dom ár ngin is ár ngoineadh, síol Éabha.

3. *Gradual*

Don't hold it against me O Christ,
That I stole
The form of your bright passion
To fashion my dream-vision

My soul's anguish,
Standing head uncovered
On the steps of the crucified city,
Is the reason for my thieving.

We are the dead who died
In Dublin and out of season,
On blasphemy's sunny day
We blew away Hiroshima.

We are no longer Gaels from the line of Ir and Éibhir,
The slaughter done in pursuit of Deirdre is no news to us.
Now, by the ship-crowded Liffey in the time of my decline
I see our beginning clear, our ending—we, children of Eve.

Translated by Aidan Hayes with Anna Ní Dhomhnaill

JUSTIN QUINN

On Speed

At night, at speed, the road is yours.
According to your will, a turn occurs.

~

At eighty miles an hour
I am an emperor.

~

We are inventing where we are.
There was no planning, there was no engineer.

~

Somewhere below the concrete tiers,
Trees are concertina'd, and would need traction for a thousand years.

~

What else should we remember
But the *autobahns* of Albert Speer?

~

On foot, they all look drugged. Prehistory
Could not have moved as slowly.

~

Cats rolled out by Cougars, Jaguars.
Jungle law, the engine roars.

~

We drive
To get ahead, to stay alive.

~

We love Japan.
We love Nissan.

~

For those who would knit bone with bone
Fresh archaeologies are often found.

~

The worries of an underwriter:
Rights and wrongs, the moral fibre.

~

A crash. A statistician's crackling graph.
Two streets off, a laugh.

PADRAIG ROONEY

In the Bonsai Garden

I dreamed of growing up
but every branch I grew
was thwarted, tampered with.
Now there's no going back.

I was contrary, and he
was there at every turn
turning me in on myself,
having his way with me.

Never a dull moment:
the braces, his funny corsets,
keeping me on my pins,
keeping me in the dark.

When I put out shoots
he'd want to know where
I was going, if I'd ever stop
playing around with myself.

I had no privacy.
Cut down to size,
stunted from the ground up,
a freak in his image.

Now I'm in my prime
he's after smaller fry
and puts me on display.
I can get up to no harm.

But overnight I dream
of flowers and fruit ripening
to a sticky fall.
A nightmare of sorts.

Sukiaki

All through those years we ate sukiaki
at anniversaries, birthdays, ends-of-terms.
We only had to say the word for our eyes
and mouths to water. The bunsen burners
whooshed under the formica tables.
We order up dishes of shrimp and squid,
beef swimming in its own blood, octopus.
We break egg white into the bubbling soup,
and keep the yolk for the dips. Cabbage
goes into the soup, onions, rice noodles.
We busy ourselves putting it all together,
dropping the squid and shrimp, the beef
into the dipping baskets, into the soup.
Then into the dishes of baby peppers,
chopped garlic, lime juice, fish sauce.
We spoon the steaming soup into bowls,
feeding each other the choicest morsels.
We hardly talk, so much do we tuck in.
The palate-shock of the first mouthful
of spicy soup. The fish and meat cooked
in their own juice. Nothing put to waste.
The soup at the end reduced to a rich stock
that lifted the roof off your mouth.

The Night Golfer

I stepped onto her fairway
breathless after too much sushi.
Those palpitations again
climbing the steps. She had
no tee, no green, no ball,
not even grass or astroturf,
but a white towel at her feet
as she gazed into the distance.
Moving neither left nor right,
she didn't answer my goodnight,
but placed her spiked shoes
on the towel and a five-iron
angled for a hole-in-one.
I stood on the landing above
and watched her perfect swing.

MARK ROPER

from **Whereabouts**

The beat of my heart
going, in the silence,
its own way.

Miraculous wound,
the roses that still flower
where a house once was.

A squashed crow's wing
lifts and waves
in the wake of a passing car.

GABRIEL ROSENSTOCK

A Handful of Haiku in Irish and English

snag breac
d'ól lán a ghoib
dá íomhá féin

magpie
sipping beakfuls
of its own image

smólach ar an bhfaiche
cigire
nóininí

thrush on the lawn
daisy
inspector

a bhfuil fágtha den oíche—
dhá phréachán
ar ghéag

all that's left of the night—
two crows
on a branch

drúcht trom...
caoineann an fear bréige
gathanna

> *heavy dew...*
> *the scarecrow*
> *weeps moonbeams*

i ngloiní dú' an daill
    dul fé
        na gréine

> *in the blind man's glasses*
> *the going down*
> *of the sun*

Mumbai,
ceirteacha ar an gcosán-
    corraíonn colainn iontu

> *Bombay,*
>   *rags on a pavement—*
>   *a body stirs in them*

ROSENSTOCK 185

Farrera (2003)

A gunsaku (haiku sequence) in Irish and English written in the Catalonian Pyrenees, April 2003

1. gaotha ag éag—
        cosán sléibhe tréigthe
                'dtí an seanséipéal

dying winds—
      faint mountain path
            to a disused church

2. timpeallaithe
        ag cama an ime—
                nach stuama é an capall

surrounded
      by so many buttercups
            how sober—the horse

3. gile Aibreáin
        deireadh an tsneachta
                á fhógairt ag an bhfiach

April sunshine—
      the raven announces
            the end of the snows

4. cuach!
  le gach glaoch
    leánn an sneachta

with each call
 the cuckoo
  melts the snow

5. an é nach ngealfaidh
 an lá amárach?
  an lá ar fad, na fáinleoga

as though tomorrow
 may never dawn—
  all day, the swallows

6. seandún?
 bualtrach
  brothall

an old fortress?
 cow dung baking
  in the sun

7. nach milis é an féar!
 an capall sléibhe
  nár sléachtadh fós

how sweet the grass!
 the mountain horse
  not yet slaughtered

8. an sruthán sléibhe
    ag brostú leis—
        cén áit?

mountain stream
    hurrying, hurrying
        where to?

9. áit éigin sa cheo
    an cloigín timpeall
        mhuineál an chapaill

somewhere in the fog
    the little bell
        around the horse's neck

10. an chuach—
    éist!
        an ag comhaireamh siollaí atá sí?

the cuckoo—
    listen!
        is she counting syllables?

11. seanfhear ag canadh sa ghort
    meallann an ghrian
        an gleann anuas

old man singing in the field
    drawing down the sun
        all over the valley

12. an mhiúil fhoighneach ina seasamh—
    cad is dóigh léi
        de na gealbhain?

the patient mule, standing,
    what does he think
        of the sparrows?

13. am bia—
    an seanóir ag canadh
        do na coiníní

feeding time—
    the old man
        singing to the rabbits

14. aon fhuaim bhriosc amháin—
    guth na ngealbhan
        sileadh an tsneachta leáite

one crisp sound—
    voices of sparrows
        dripping of melting snow

15. aer tanaí an tsléibhe
    gach áit: sna gága
        gallchnó folamh

thin mountain air
    everywhere: rock crevices
        empty walnut shell

16. cnoic faoi shneachta—
    béal an tsearraigh
        breac le bainne na lárach

snowcapped hills—
    the foal's mouth
        flecked with mare's milk

17. a sheanchloig
        i dtúr Farrera de Pallars—
            cathain a labhróidh tú arís?

old tower-bell
    in Farrera de Pallars—
        when will you speak again?

18. an t-iora rua
        (ar chrann nach n-aithním)
            tá deartháir aige ag baile

the squirrel
    (on a tree I do not know)
        has a brother in my land

19. an cnagaire adhmaid
        is máistir é
            fiú roimh eadara

the woodpecker—
    first thing at morning—
        is a master

20. taoi amuigh ansan,
    áit éigin, i do thost,
        a shionnaigh shleamhain

you are out there,
    somewhere, on silent feet,
        wily fox

21. cén fáth ar dheis?
    cén fáth ar chlé?
        féachaint shaonta an ghealbhain

why look to the left,
    the right?—impossible to say,
        the simple sparrow

22. na héadaí a fágadh
    ar an líne: athbheoite
        ag bailc úr sléibhe

clothes left on the line
    have been revived—
        pure mountain rain

23. scamaill dhubha
    ag triall ar an gcéad ghleann eile—
        cumhracht an chaife láidir

dark clouds leaving
    for the next valley—
        aroma of strong coffee

24. leathanach bán
    agus sneachta Farrera—
        nach léir í an Úrchríoch

facing a blank page
    and the snows of Farrera—
        Pure Land is clear

25. litríocht á plé
    an oíche go léir:
        tostmhar an fíon sa ghloine

talking literature all night
    the wine in the glass
        becomes still

26. gíoscán na gclár urláir—
    tuairisc ar chogadh
        i gcéin

creaking of floor boards—
    reports of a war
        far away

27. meán oíche—
    níl gíocs ó chloigín
        an chapaill sléibhe

midnight—
    no sound
        from the horse's bell

28. maidin ghlas
    crobh iolair
        tairneáilte sa doras

chilly morning
    an eagle's talon
        nailed to the door

29. uan aonair ag méileach
    an fhuaim
        á seachadadh ag na sléibhte

a lone lamb bleating
    the sound carried
        from mountain to mountain

RICHARD RYAN

Five Senryū (18th century)

"So she's only got
one eye, but
cripes, what an eye!"—
the marriage broker.

Settling down to
the breast feed:
"I think there's a sardine
in the pantry—help yourself!"

A flying fart!
No fun, though, like this—
all alone.

That horse, farting—
four, now five noses
wrinkling along the river ferry.

Have they no homes
To go to?—the bride
Creeping out for a night pee.

JOHN W. SEXTON

Issa in the golden corridor
(Kobayashi Issa, 1763-1827)

In his dream Issa
pulls a turnip from the ground,
unravels the world.

Clods of earth rise up
to smother the sun. The sea
turns the sky to mud.

Issa wakes in sweat.
The crickets on the grass floor
sing out to rouse him

"Oh, my good children
you've rescued Papa Issa.
The world was undone."

Issa lies sleepless.
Damp night fills his hut with fog,
foxes pass his door.

In the cold morning
he takes snails to the graveyard
for lack of flowers.

Upon each gravestone
a snail leaves silver prayers.
Issa, happy, weeps.

Plums rot on the trees.
Issa shows them to the wasps
that cling to his sleeve.

"I'll try one myself,
oh little samurai wasp."
Issa eats a plum.

Surrounded by wasps
Issa gorges himself, spits
out twenty plum stones.

Later's Issa's gut
is angry. Foolish Issa.
He gets a fever.

The plums fill his mind
with golden fog, take him down
to the wasp spirits.

"You stole all our plums,"
hisses the Lord of Wasps. Then
Issa wakes again.

EILEEN SHEEHAN

claiming it

having failed to find
Reclariant in the dictionary
I've decided to claim it
as my personal invention

if I were Japanese I would render it
in a few elegant strokes

the pictogram would denote

> woman leaning back in chair
> having studied her life at length
> is seeing things clearly again

usage would also permit
its application in Biology
when referring to
an advanced stage of recovery
following cardiac procedures

the way ten thousand shadows
darkening the sky can mean
a multitude of fledglings
reveling in flight

JAMES SIMMONS

Empire

Portrush encroaches on the land of the rising sun!
There is still scope for the vicar's younger son.
After the family crisis in Kerr Street
in the 60s, this boy has landed on his feet,
settled in Tokyo, no less, not spewing
up his guts in the gutter, not him,
but editing haiku magazines, reviewing
the local poets, a modern Lord Jim.
Respected, he rises to lecture them
on Ulster poetry, 'Fact, Faction and Feud'.
He is helping a gay network create
scope for their talents, negotiate
life in exile and find it good;
fitting into or taking over beds
and boards in the ancient Orient, aglow…
while former neighbours still shake their heads
over what happened twenty years ago.

PETER SIRR

In the Japanese Garden

The little red bridges
Have nothing to tell
Of exact endearments,

Kimonos rustling in the breeze.
The fate of millions
Was never settled here

Though the rare flowers bow
And in the hierarchic waterfall
Every drop knows its place.

A Wicklow wind clicks
In bamboo that has never hurried
Through staked-out prisoners

And if we can never replace
The inscrutable shoguns
Who should be here

Babbling of honour among
The fag-ends and Coke tins
Our local samurai

Are coming on.
More and more accurately
They test their penknives

And their girls
On the educational exotica,
In the peeling pagodas.

GERARD SMYTH

December Moon

The December moon like an alabaster mask
lords it over the long night.
It illuminates the gravel path,
looks into the mirror in my room
and leaves its cold breath there.

A moon that lights weed-covered yards
and the ruins of Clonmacnoise.
It is chained to the hours of slow time,
creeps through temple and church
and knows where the crime was done.

It shines into the cradle,
appears through rain in the cemetery:
same orb that Bashō saw
in the garden, above his cherry tree.

BILL TINLEY

Jeanne Hébuterne

> *Nata a Parigi il 6 Aprile 1898*
> *Morta a Parigi il 25 Gennaio 1920*
> *Di Amedeo Modigliani compagna*
> *Devota fina all'extremo sacrifizio*

In the painter's eye
Your face is oblong,
Sharp as a varnished finger-nail or nib;
Blinded by his hand
Your Japanese head
Is angled in the shadow of beauty.

Your crescent ear-ring,
Your waning neckline,
The miniscule curves of your silent lips
Are simply brush-strokes
On the naked cloth.
You escape us on your lover's canvas.

History dissolves
You like a pigment
Lost in the background of its masterpiece,
A minor detail
In a catalogue
Of kings, *conquistadors*, carnage, crime.

Your name's *staccato*,
Your blurred photograph,
The foreign tongue above your resting-place,
The mixed-up colours
Of your eyes and hair,
The mistaken date of your leap to death—

Nothing accurate
Secures you or stems
Oblivion except your final act,
Your pact of passion.
Amongst the crumpled
Curves and definitions of your body

In its pavement pose
Art has no domain;
The oils and water-colours crack and fade
Past recognition
While you, luminous
But blemished, find your medium at last,

Cradling your baby
In the one embrace
Of birth and death. Let your broken figure
Be your signature
On life, the emblem
Of a love no conspiracy can frame.

JOSEPH WOODS

Sailing to Hokkaido

After dinner
walk to the stern alone

and look out
for the time it takes

to discern two
darknesses from one.

Suiheisen was the line
where sky and sea met.

For two horizons,
sky and sea

land and sky
there are two words.

Tonight one darkness
overruns another.

There is no line between
the two. Walk back

to the palpable heartbeat
of a generator.

Where the Word for Beautiful is Clean

What brought me out that morning
was the sound of someone on the roof

a monkey glanced down, then stared
away at the something interesting,

eating the core of a stolen apple,
hungry and halfway down its mountain.

I turned to see, snows had arrived
and Kyoto was below in its dip

surrounded by mountains gone white
overnight. For miles between,

millions of roof tiles covered and clean.

New Year's Day, Nagasaki

Cats have a place in this city,
you can smell them everywhere
and it's good to smell animals
again, even cats.

Or watch them fold into corners
hunting sun in a cemetery
full of offerings; sandalwood
incense, sprays of anise and sake.

At the church of the twenty six
martyrs, you light candles
I wait at the back and watch.

In this light
the light on you,
you move to give
worship a meaning.

I turn to a bay of ships
through a green
and then blue window.

Triptych

I

From the kitchen of mild odours
a simple meal of rice, beans and miso soup.

Each monk has his own set of eating bowls
which he takes care of, pouring hot water

into each bowl to drink the rinse, so as not to waste
a particle of food. In praise for the minute lives

sacrificed, the time and energy expended.

In the kitchen garlic and onions,
flavours that affect the spirit, are forbidden.

II

Every leaf is heavy here with rain
and a scent of mould rises to muzzle.

Stone lanterns are quenched by the hood of moss . . .

*—Stay long enough and the seasons will create
the same vacillations they would at home.*

III

Under a monk's calm instruction
I light three sticks of incense,

for God, my ancestors and me.

—*Things are lost because of my English,*
he says.

Because of *my* Japanese and my English.

Persimmon

Before
    the tepid jolt
of departure
from Kutsukawa,
the eye catches
a persimmon tree
out of leaf
and persimmons
more orange
for the absence
of leaf.
What is it
with fruit that
takes the frosts
to ripen?

MACDARA WOODS

Rosbeg, July 2nd, 1970

The mouth is open, taste awash,
the raw wind howls upon the roof,
scythes the soldiering nettles;
and dark drives boats to fear and sea.
The road bends; dark nuns approach me
under a stern St. Joseph's stare
(while wire will hymn without benefit of clergy)
and, we smile, then pause for civil greeting :
'a shop?' 'yes Sister, down the road'
& I'm treading the egg-shell path for a drink.

I find a cadence in this countryside
—washed white flat Japanese light;
the straight haired figures of a yellow print—
and so I'm nearing happy, though I can't decide
whether it be rock, or space, or wind
that filters through the mind.

AFTERWORD

Petals on a Bough

SEAMUS HEANEY

The following is an edited version of the introduction to a reading of 'Japanese effect' poems (many of which appear in this anthology) given in Dublin on November 15, 2000. The remarks and the reading were presented as that year's Lafcadio Hearn Lecture, at a meeting sponsored by the Japan-Ireland Society.

Poetry is a domestic art, most itself when most at home. It has even been argued, famously, that poetry is what is lost in translation. But while it is true that poets depend for the most part on the hearth-life and home-sweet-homeness of their native tongue, they also tend to be the Oliver Twists of language, never satisfied with their allotted ration, always asking for more, inclined to feel that enough is not enough but only the start of it, that somewhere there is another word that will be the key to another world.

So when native traditions are rejuvenated by what we now call 'the shock of the new', it is often through contact with a foreign culture that the new possibilities suggest themselves. This, after all, is what happened in Japanese poetry at the end of the nineteenth century, when the so called *shintaishi* or New-Style Poetry began to be written. The introduction to *The Penguin Book of Japanese Verse* attributes this radical shift of style to the publication in 1882 of a volume of translations of miscellaneous English verse, including excerpts from work by Longfellow, Tennyson, Shakespeare's *Henry IV, Part 2*, and *Hamlet*. The volume also included experimental poems by the compilers and it was followed seven years later by another such anthology entitled *Omokage* (Semblances) which again featured translations of work by Shakespeare and several figures from the European Romantic movement including Byron, Goethe and Heine.

I don't know if William Wordsworth was among the Romantic poets translated in those epoch-making anthologies, but Wordsworth is where I want to begin. It seems to me that the scenes which inspired his most characteristic poetry could well have inspired many of the great masters of Japan. The English and Japanese sensibilities respond in similar ways to the natural world, and landscapes which brought out the best in Wordsworth could equally well have provided the setting for a haiku by Bashō. Significantly also, the English poet's work abounds in phrases which could be used to describe the general emotional impact of a certain kind of Japanese lyric—as when he speaks of being 'an inmate of this active universe', of being taught to feel 'the self-sufficing power of solitude' or a something in nature which is 'far more deeply interfused', and so on.

What is un-Japanese about Wordsworth, however—and you only need to remember a poem like *The Prelude* or 'Tintern Abbey' to realize it—is the nimbus of introspection and ratiocination which surrounds the physical details of the scene. In this Romantic period, poetry in English typically allows itself greater scope for commentary and elucidation, tending to clarify where Japanese poetry would be content to imply; often eager to point out where Japanese poetry would be happy to sink in; tending to add where the Japanese would subtract.

Consider, for example, the following passage from *The Prelude*. Wordsworth is remembering a schoolboy expedition that he and his companions once made on horseback, a daytrip when they galloped off to visit the ruins of Furness Abbey on the shores of Cumberland. Once there, they absorb the atmosphere of the place, the carved stone effigies of knights and abbots scattered about the roofless chantry, the wind passing overhead and the sound of the sea ebbing and flowing in the background—until it is time for them to go back. Then:

> Our steeds remounted, and the summons given,
> With whip and spur we by the chantry flew
> In uncouth race, and left the cross-legged knight
> And the stone abbot, and that single wren
> Which one day sang so sweetly in the nave
> Of the old church that, though from recent showers
> The earth was comfortless, and, touched by faint
> Internal breezes, from the roofless walls
> The shuddering ivy dripped large drops, yet still
> So sweetly mid the gloom the invisible bird
> Sang to itself that there I could have made
> My dwelling place, and lived forever there,
> To hear such music.

The dripping ivy, the roofless walls, the song of a single wren: a Japanese poet is likely to have been content with those elements of the scene. He would have been drawn to the still centre of the moment. The narrative would probably have fallen away, or perhaps have been reported in a brief anecdotal prose interlude. Typically, the moment of pure perception would have been isolated, the psychological and philosophical implications remaining unspoken. What Wordsworth explicitly declares—'I could have...lived for ever there/To hear such music' the Japanese poet would most likely have suggested by one or two illuminating images.

Still, English poetry would soon enough learn the Japanese lesson. Only a couple of decades after the 'new-style poets' of the 1890s brought out their anthologies in Japan, new-style poems began to appear in little publications in London. By the second decade of the twentieth century two Americans had arrived and were producing work that would leave its mark on much of the verse written in English since. Ezra Pound and T. S. Eliot landed as expatriates, seeking on the one hand to find in Europe the origins of their cultural tradition, and seeking on the other hand to shake that tradition up, revive it and retune it to other registers. It was Pound who produced the work that here concerns us most, when he wrote one of the briefest but most influential poems in his total *oeuvre,* the well known 'In a Station of the Metro'. In one stroke, or rather two lines, Pound managed to banish, as it were, his inner Wordsworth, and demonstrated to others that they could do the same.

His famous note about the composition of 'In a Station of the Metro' tells how he had attempted to find words for sensations that he had experienced after a unique and mysterious vision of beautiful faces coming and going among the passengers in the Paris métro at Place de la Concorde. 'There came an equation ...' Pound wrote, 'not in speech, but in little splotches of colour.' He had begun by composing a thirty line poem but had destroyed it because it didn't achieve a satisfactory intensity of expression; six months then passed and he wrote one half that length; and a year later he produced what he called a '*hokku*-like sentence':

The apparition of these faces in the crowd:
Petals on a wet, black bough.

'I dare say it is meaningless,' Pound concluded, 'unless one has drifted into a certain vein of thought. In a poem of this sort one is trying to record the precise instant when a thing outward and objective transforms itself, or darts into a thing inward and subjective.'

The poem is far from meaningless, and it is largely thanks to its existence that readers (and writers) in English have drifted 'into a certain vein of thought'. Thanks to these fourteen words, we are now well attuned to the Japanese effect, the evocation of that precise instant of perception, and are ready to grant such evocation of the instant a self-sufficiency of its own. We don't require any labouring of the point. We are happy if the image sets off its own echoes and associations, if it speaks indirectly, as Issa speaks in his haiku: 'A good world——/dew drops fall/by ones by twos.'

By ones, by twos, ripples pulsed out from the image poem, so it was inevitable, especially given Pound's capacities as an operator on the literary scene, that the new Japanese effect should be integrated into the history of poetry in English as 'The Imagist Movement'. Moreover, once the aesthetic procedure was named it was to a certain extent tamed, and like any other domesticated species, it began to breed and be taken for granted in its new setting—as in this other early example of the genre by T. E. Hulme:

> Old houses were scaffolding once
> And workmen whistling.

Neither Pound's poem nor Hulme's obeys the formal rules of the Japanese; the syllable count of 5-7-5 is neglected and the 'seasonal' word is missing, but the sense of evanescence, of the transitoriness of things, of the stillness behind things into which they eventually pass, this essential quality is nevertheless present.

It might even be said that with the writing of these early image-based poems and with the formulation of the principles of imagism, the concept of *mono no aware* enters the English language, both in theory and in practice. *Mono no aware* is defined in a glossary of Japanese artistic terms as

> a literary and artistic ideal cultivated in the Heian period. Literally meaning 'pathos of things', it usually refers to sadness or melancholy arising from a deep empathic appreciation of the ephemeral beauty manifested in nature, human life or a work of art.

For curiosity, I went through the recently published *New Penguin Book of English Verse* in search of this effect in pre-Imagist periods, but didn't discover anything. This is not to say, of course, that poetry in English is unaware or unexpressive of the underlife of feelings or the melancholy of things: since Anglo-Saxon times the elegiac mood has been a constant of the poetic literature. It's just that the means of expression are different. In 1869, for example, Matthew Arnold wrote this brief, untitled poem:

> Below the surface-stream, shallow and light,
> Of what we say we feel—below the stream,
> As light, of what we think we feel—there flows
> With noiseless current strong, obscure and deep,
> The central stream of what we feel indeed.

What the haiku/imagist form can do is to reach down into that noiseless, strong, obscure, deep central stream and give both poet and reader a sense of epiphany. It's worth noticing indeed that the word 'epiphany' becomes available as a literary term around about the time when Pound is coining the term 'imagism', James Joyce being the one who was responsible for this new extension and application of its meaning. In their different ways, Pound and Joyce felt a need to extend the alphabet of expressiveness, and found a way to articulate what T. S. Eliot would call 'the notion of some infinitely gentle / Infinitely suffering thing'—a thing which was also for Eliot inherent in certain 'images': 'I am moved by fancies that are curled/ Around these images and cling.'

In the years since these early developments, the haiku form and the generally Japanese effect have been a constant feature of poetry in English. The names of Bashō and Issa and Buson have found their way into our discourse to the extent that we in Ireland have learnt to recognize something Japanese in the earliest lyrics of the native tradition. The hermit poets who wrote in Old Irish in the little monasteries were also masters of the precise and suggestive:

> Int én bec
> ro léc feit
> do rinn guip
>   glanbuidi:
> fo-ceird fáid
> ós Loch Laíg
> Ion do chraíb
>   chairdbuidi.
>   —*9th century Irish*

The small bird
let a chirp
from its beak:
    I heard
woodnotes, whin-
gold, sudden:
the Lagan
    blackbird.

The economy of means, the sense of a huge encircling stillness, of swiftness and transience all at once, these qualities recall equally the traditional *haiku* and the twentieth century imagist poem, and this single example will have to stand for many other lyrics that could be cited from the Old Irish canon.

Another quality which the Old Irish poet shares with his Japanese counterpart is a quality we might call 'this worldness'—both are as alert as hunters to their physical surroundings—and yet there is also a strong sense of another world within this 'this worldness', one to which poetic expression promises access. In each case, it's as if the poet is caught between the delights of the contingent and the invitations of the transcendent, yet by registering as precisely and poignantly as possible his consciousness of this middle state he manages to effect what Matthew Arnold would have called 'a criticism of life'. So you could argue that there is a direct line running from the startle of recognition in the work of the early Christian hermit as he renders the whole strangeness of the blackbird's song to the 'tinkle of china / And tea into china' as Derek Mahon contrasts the exquisite manners of those attending the snow party (in his poem of that name) with the savagery of contemporary European wars, including those being waged in Ireland 'in the service of barbarous kings'. Mahon's poem, one of the most durable written in the late twentieth century, constitutes in effect a proof of the contention by his friend Michael Longley—that other Hiberno-Japanese master—that the opposite of war is not peace but civilization.

Yet Japanese poetry is not all snow parties and snow water. One of its most attractive features is the folk form known as *senryū*, more humorous and robust than the *haiku,* more down to earth and insinuating, and again you could make interesting juxtapositions of *senryū,* with the Old Irish triads—or with brief merry poems by Iain Crichton Smith written first in Scots Gaelic and translated into English as 'Gaelic Stories', or with Paul Muldoon's 'Hopewell Haiku', or Michael Hartnett's 'Inchicore Haiku' or Cathal Ó Searcaigh's glosses from Gortahork.

So while it is true that our sense of the Japanese effect was heightened by Ezra Pound's Imagism, it's also fair to say that from the start there has been a certain resemblance between vernacular Irish and traditional Japanese ways of looking at things. And it can be further said that in the course of the twentieth century, as empires and ideologies contended for supremacy, and atrocities were committed on a scale unprecedented in human history, poets became desperately aware of the dangers of rhetoric and abstraction. In these circumstances, the poet's duty to be truthful became more and more imperative, and as it did the chastity and reticence of Japanese poetry grew more and more attractive. Its closeness to common experience and its acknowledgement of mystery, its sensitivity to *lacrimae rerum,* to the grievous aspects of human experience, have made it a permanent and ever more valuable resource to which other literatures can turn.

ABOUT THE EDITORS

IRENE DE ANGELIS graduated on Yeats's Nō plays and received a PhD from the University of Turin with a dissertation on the "Japanese Effect" in contemporary Irish poetry. With Prof. David Ewick, of the Chuo University Tokyo, she is co-editor of *Emerging from Absence: Archive of Japan in English-Language Verse,* http://www.themargins.net/archive.html (2003 onwards). In 2004 she went on a study-tour of Japan. She is currently preparing a monograph on the Ireland-Japan literary connection.

JOSEPH WOODS was born in Drogheda in 1966. He lived in Kyoto from 1991 to 1993 and was first published in Japan. His collections are *Sailing to Hokkaido* (2001) and *Bearings* (2005), both from Worple Press, UK. He received the Patrick Kavanagh Award in 2000 and is currently Director of Poetry Ireland.

NOTES ON CONTRIBUTORS

FERGUS ALLEN was born in Ireland in 1921 but has lived in England for many years. Of his four collections of poems, *Gas Light & Coke* (Dedalus Press, 2006) is the most recent.

DERMOT BOLGER was born in Finglas, Co. Dublin in 1959 and founded and edited the Raven Arts Press in Dublin. A novelist, playwright and poet, his poetry collections include *The Chosen Moment* (New Island Books, 2004). He is a member of Aosdána.

PAT BORAN was born in Portlaoise in 1963. He lives in Dublin where he is Editor of The Dedalus Press and presenter of The Poetry Programme on RTÉ Radio 1. His *New and Selected Poems* appeared from Salt Publishing in 2005. He is a member of Aosdána. His personal website is at www.patboran.com

DAVID BURLEIGH was born in Northern Ireland in 1950 and has lived in Tokyo for almost thirty years. He has collaborated on translations from Japanese of poetry and haiku, and is the editor of *Helen Waddell's Writings from Japan* (Irish Academic Press, 2005).

PADDY BUSHE was born in Dublin in 1948 and is the author of seven collections in English and Irish, as well as three books of translations. His *New and Selected Poems* is due from Dedalus early in 2008.

RUTH CARR was born in Belfast in 1953. She was joint editor of *The Honest Ulsterman* and edited the anthology *The Female Line* (1985). Her first collection was *There is a House* (Summer Palace Press, 1999), and she is nearing completion of a second collection.

CIARAN CARSON was born in 1948 in Belfast, where he is Professor of Poetry at Queen's University. He has published nine collections including *First Language*, winner of the 1993 T.S. Eliot Prize, and *Breaking News*, winner of the 2003 Forward Prize. His translation of the Irish epic *The Táin* is published by Penguin Classics in 2007. He is a member of Aosdána.

DEIRDRE CARTMILL'S collection *Midnight Solo* (2004) was published by Lagan Press. Her poetry has been published widely in journals and anthologies. She has written for television and radio and won awards for her scriptwriting. She lives in Belfast.

JUANITA CASEY was born in England of Irish parents in 1925. She has written fiction and short stories, and her poetry collection *Eternity Smith* was published in 1985.

AUSTIN CLARKE was born in Dublin in 1896. He lectured in English at UCD and moved to London in 1937. He published many volumes of poetry, numerous plays, as well as several novels. He died in 1974. His *Selected Poems* were published by The Lilliput Press in 1991.

PATRICK COTTER was born in 1963 in Cork. He has published several chapbooks, as well as the 1990 collection *The Mysogynist's Blue Nightmare* (Raven Arts Press). He is director the Munster Literature Centre and Editor of the Irish section of Poetry International.

YVONNE CULLEN lives in Dublin where she writes and teaches writing. Her first collection of poems, *Invitation to the Air* (Italics Press, 1998), won the American Ireland Fund Award in 1997.

TONY CURTIS was born in Dublin in 1955. He is the author of seven collections of poetry, most recently *The Well in the Rain: New and Selected Poems* (Arc Publications, 2006). He has been awarded the Irish National Poetry Prize and is a member of Aosdána.

GERALD DAWE was born in Belfast in 1952. He visited Japan in 2005 as a guest of IASIL-Japan. A Fellow of Trinity College Dublin, his most recent books include *Lake Geneva* (The Gallery Press, 2003) and *The Proper Word: Collected Criticism* (Creighton University Press, 2007).

PATRICK DEELEY was born in Loughrea, Co. Galway in 1953 and now lives in Dublin, where he works as a primary school principal. He has written four collections of poetry, most recently *Decoding Samara* (Dedalus Press, 2000), and is preparing a fifth. He is also the author of four prose works for young readers published by O'Brien.

GREG DELANTY was born in Cork in 1958 and now teaches at St. Michael's College in Vermont. He has received numerous awards, most recently a Guggenheim for Poetry. His most recent book is *Collected Poems 1986-2006* (Carcanet Press).

MOYRA DONALDSON was born in Co. Down in 1956. She has published four collections of poetry, most recently *The Horse's Nest* (Lagan Press, 2006). She also writes for stage and screen and has edited a number of anthologies.

KATIE DONOVAN spent her early youth in Co. Wexford and now lives in Dublin. She has published three collections of poetry: *Watermelon Man*, *Entering the Mare*, and *Day of the Dead*, all with Bloodaxe Books. She is currently Writer-in-Residence with Dun Laoghaire/Rathdown County Council and IADT.

MARY DORCEY was born in Dublin in 1950. Both a poet and a novelist, in 2001 she published her collection *Like Joy in Season, Like Sorrow* (Salmon Poetry).

KATHERINE DUFFY was born in Dundalk, Co. Luth in 1962. Her first collection is *The Erratic Behaviour of Tides* (Dedalus Press, 1998). She has also published a novel in Irish for teenagers, *Splanctha!* (Cló Iar-Chonnachta, 1997). She lives in Dublin.

SEÁN DUNNE was born in Waterford in 1956. He graduated from UCC and worked as a columnist for *The Cork Examiner*. His collections include *The Sheltered Nest* (1992) and *Time and The Island* (1996). Dunne died in 1995. His *Collected Poems* were published by The Gallery Press in 2005.

PAUL DURCAN was born in Dublin in 1944. His most recent collections are *Cries of an Irish Caveman* (The Harvill Press, 2001) and *The Art of Life* (The Harvill Press, 2004). He visited Japan in 2004 and is a member of Aosdána.

DESMOND EGAN was born in Athlone in 1936. He has published 18 collections of poems, as well as volumes of prose and translation. He spent a semester as Poet-in-Residence in Kansai University, Osaka in 1997. He is Artistic Director of the Gerard Manley Hopkins Summer School.

JOHN ENNIS was born in Westmeath in 1944. He has published several poetry collections, including *Near St. Mullins* (Dedalus Press, 2002) and *Goldcrest Falling* (Scop Productions Inc., 2006) and has co-edited two major anthologies of poetry from Ireland and Newfoundland, the most recent of which is *The Echoing Years* (Waterford Institute of Technology, 2007).

PETER FALLON was born in 1951. He founded The Gallery Press in 1970. His most recent books are *News of the World: Selected and New Poems* (1998), *The Georgics of Virgil* (2004 / Oxford World Classics, 2006) and *The Company of Horses* (2007). With Derek Mahon he has edited *The Penguin Book of Contemporary Irish Poetry* (1990). He is a member of Aosdána.

GERARD FANNING was born in Dublin in 1952. A graduate of UCD, he has published three collections of poems: *Easter Snow* (1992), *Working for the Government* (1999) and *Water & Power* (2004), all with The Dedalus Press.

ANDREW FITZSIMONS was born in Dublin in 1965. Since 1998 he has lived in Tokyo, where he teaches at Gakushuin University. A study of Thomas Kinsella, *The Sea of Disappointment*, is forthcoming from UCD Press.

ANTHONY GLAVIN won the Patrick Kavanagh Poetry Competition in 1987. His collection, *The Wrong Side of The Alps*, was published by The Gallery Press in 1989. The poems here are from his ambitious unfinished sequence, 'Living In Hiroshima', the first three sections of which were published in his Gallery collection. He died in 2006.

MARK GRANIER has published two collections with Salmon Poetry, *Airborne* (2001) and *The Sky Road* (2007). His awards include a first prize in the UK New Writer Poetry Competition in 1997 and the Vincent Buckley Prize in 2004. He lives in Dublin.

PAMELA GREENE was born in Belfast where she works as a lawyer. A pamphlet of poems, *Heartland*, was published by Lapwing Press in 1998, and her collection *Tattoo Me* was published by Summer Palace Press in 2002.

EAMON GRENNAN was born in Dublin in 1941. His most recent collections are *Still Life With Waterfall* (2002) and *The Quick of It* (2004), both from The Gallery Press. His forthcoming collection is entitled *Out of Breath*.

MAURICE HARMON was born in Co. Dublin in 1930. An academic and a poet, he spent a year as visiting professor of English at Kobe College. His collection of poems *The Last Regatta* (Salmon Poetry, 2000), includes a section written during that time.

MICHAEL HARTNETT was born in Co. Limerick in 1941. He published a number of collections in Irish and English, including *A Farewell to English* (1975) and *Inchicore Haiku* (1985). He died in 1999. *Collected Poems* was published by The Gallery Press in 2002.

FRANCIS HARVEY was born in Enniskillen in 1925 and now lives in Donegal. He has published four collections of poems, including *Making Space: New & Selected Poems* (Dedalus Press, 2001) and *Collected Poems* (Dedalus Press, 2007).

SEAMUS HEANEY was born in Co. Derry in 1939. He was awarded the Nobel Prize for Literature in 1995. He has been Ralph Waldo Emerson Poet-in-Residence at Harvard University. His most recent collection is *District and Circle* (Faber & Faber, 2006). Following a first visit in 1987, he visited Japan in 1990 and 1998. He is a member of Aosdána.

RACHAEL HEGARTY was born in Dublin in 1968. She was educated at the University of Massachusetts, Boston and Trinity College Dublin. She lived in Shimane, Japan from 1996 to 1999. Her poems have been widely published.

JOHN HEWITT was born in Belfast in 1907. He was appointed Writer-in-Residence at Queen's University in 1976 and was made Freeman of the City of Belfast in 1983. He died in 1987. His *Selected Poems* were published by Blackstaff Press in 2007.

JOHN HUGHES was born in Belfast in 1962. His collections include *Negotiations with the Chill Wind* (1991), *The Devil Himself* (1996), and *The Something in Particular* (1986). His most recent collection is *Fast Forward* (Lagan Press, 2003). He lives in Donegal with his family.

PEARSE HUTCHINSON was born in Glasgow in 1927 and moved to Dublin in 1932. He recently published his *Collected Poems* (The Gallery Press, 2002). He has translated from Catalan and Galico-Portoguese, and, with Melita Cataldi, he has written Italian versions of Old Irish Poetry.

BIDDY JENKINSON was born 1949. Her recent collections include *An Grá Riabhach* (Coscéim, 1999); and *Rogha Dánta* (Cork University Press, 1999). Her play *Mise, Subhó agus Maccó* was produced by Aisling Ghéar. She has recently been in Tokyo visiting family and friends.

FRED JOHNSTON was born in Belfast in 1951. With Neil Jordan and Peter Sheridan, he was co-founder of the Irish Writers' Co-operative in the Seventies and founder of the Cúirt festival in 1986. His collection *The Oracle Room* is forthcoming from Cinnamon Press. He currently lives in Galway.

EILEEN KATO was born in 1932 in Erris, Co. Mayo and has lived in Japan for fifty years. She is the widow of Ambassador Yoshiya Kato. She has published widely in journals. Her major translations include Shiba Ryotarō's *The Heart Remembers Home / Kokyō Bojigataku Soro*, and *Drunk as a Lord / Yotte Sorō* (Kodansah International, 2001).

NEVILLE KEERY was born in 1939. He returned to his native Dublin in 2001 after a career with the European Commission in Brussels, which included a short professional visit to a conference in Kyoto. His second collection of poems, *Home*, is to appear this year.

THOMAS KINSELLA was born in Dublin in 1928. His most recent collections are *Man of War* (2007) and *Belief and Unbelief* (2007), both from Dedalus Press. In 2006 he was awarded an Honorary Degree by the University of Turin. In June 2007 he was made Freeman of the City of Dublin.

MATT KIRKHAM lives in the Ards peninsula, Co. Down and was featured in Lagan Press's *Poetry Introductions 1*. His first collection, *The Lost Museums* (Lagan Press, 2006), won the Rupert and Eithne Strong Award.

ANATOLY (ANTHONY) KUDRYAVITSKY was born in 1954 in Moscow of a Polish father and half-Irish mother. His latest publication is *Morning at Mount Ring*, a collection of his haiku and senryu (Doghouse, 2007).

MICHAEL LONGLEY was born in Belfast in 1939. His collections include *The Weather in Japan* (2000) and *Snow Water* (2004). His *Collected Poems* were published in 2006 by Jonathan Cape. Longley visited Japan in 1991 to give a series of readings and lectures. He is a member of Aosdána.

BRIAN LYNCH was born in Dublin in 1945. He is a poet, novelist, and screenwriter. He has never been to Japan but has studied and sometimes practised Zen. His latest novel, *The Winner of Sorrow* (New Island Books, 2005) was nominated for the Hughes & Hughes Novel of the Year Award. He is a member of Aosdána.

DEREK MAHON was born in Belfast in 1941. His most recent publications include *Collected Poems* (1999) and *Harbour Lights* (2005), both from The Gallery Press. He was the recipient of the David Cohen Prize for Literature in 2007 and is a member of Aosdána.

AIDAN CARL MATHEWS was born in Dublin in 1956. His poetry collections include *According to the Small Hours* (Jonathan Cape, 1998); his plays include *Exit/Entrance* (The Gallery Press, 1990); and he has also published collections of stories and a novel. His awards include The Patrick Kavanagh Award (1976) and Academy of American Poets Award (1982).

JOHN McAULIFFE is from Listowel. He is the author of *A Better Life* (2002) and *Next Door* (2007), both published by the Gallery Press. He lives in Manchester where he co-directs the University of Manchester's Centre for New Writing.

JAMES McCABE was born in Dublin in 1966. He holds a doctorate in poetry from Oxford University. 'Cliara Hiaku' is from his collection *The White Battlefield of Silence* (Dedalus Press, 1999) and is inspired by correspondences between Japanese and Gaelic traditional forms.

THOMAS McCARTHY was born in Co. Waterford in 1954 and educated at UCC. He has worked as a librarian in Cork for thirty years. His most recent book, *Merchant Prince* (2005), was published by Anvil Press Poetry. He is a member of Aosdána.

MEDBH McGUCKIAN was born in Belfast in 1950. Her collections of poetry include *The Face of the Earth* (The Gallery Press, 2002), *Had I a Thousand Lives* (The Gallery Press, 2003), and *The Book of the Angel* (The Gallery Press, 2004). She visited Japan with her son in 1998 and is a member of Aosdána.

PETER McMILLAN lives in Tokyo, Japan, where he teaches and works as an art dealer specializing in contemporary art. He is also a painter, and his gallery can be seen at www.mcmillanart.com.

TED McNULTY was born in New York of Irish parents. A news reporter and university lecturer, he spent the latter part of his life in Dublin. His two collections are *Rough Landings* (1992) and *On the Block* (1995), both from Salmon Poetry. He died in Dublin in 1998.

PAULA MEEHAN was born in Dublin in 1955. She is a poet and playwright, and her poetry collections include *Dharmakaya* (Carcanet Press, 2000). Her awards include the Butler Literary Award (1998), and the Denis Devlin Award (2002). She is a member of Aosdána.

DOROTHY MOLLOY was born in Ballina. She was educated at UCD and worked as a historical researcher and painter. Her collections are *Hare Soup* (Faber & Faber, 2004) and *Gethsemane Day* (Faber & Faber, 2006). She died in 2004.

SINÉAD MORRISSEY was born in Belfast in 1972. She is the author of three collections: *There Was Fire in Vancouver* (1996), *Between Here and There* (2002) and *The State of the Prisons* (2005), all published by Carcanet. Her awards include the Patrick Kavanagh Award, the Rupert and Eithne Strong Award and the Michael Hartnett Poetry Prize. She lived in Japan from 1995 to 1997.

PAUL MULDOON was born in Co. Armagh in 1951. His most recent collections include the Pulitzer Prize-winning *Moy Sand and Gravel* (Faber & Faber, 2002) and *Horse Latitudes* (Faber & Faber, 2006). Currently he is Howard Clark '21 University Professor in the Humanities at Princeton University. He visited Japan in 1994. He is a member of Aosdána.

GERRY MURPHY was born in Cork in 1952. Among his published collections are *Extracts from the Lost Log-book of Christopher Columbus* (Dedalus Press, 1999), *Torso of an Ex-Girlfriend* (Dedalus Press, 2003) and *End of Part One: New and Selected Poems* (Dedalus Press, 2006).

NUALA Ní DHOMHNAILL was born in 1952 in Lancashire. In 1957 her family moved back to Ireland. She is an Irish-language poet. Her next book *The Fifty Minute Mermaid*, translated by Paul Muldoon, is due out from The Gallery Press in October. She has visited Japan many times and is a member of Aosdána.

JULIE O'CALLAGHAN was born in Chicago in 1954 and has lived in Ireland since 1974. Her latest collection of poetry for adults is *No Can Do* (Bloodaxe Books, 2000), for which she was awarded the Michael Hartnett Poetry Prize. Her poems for older children have appeared in numerous anthologies in the UK. She is a member of Aosdána.

JOHN O'DONNELL was born in 1960. He has published two poetry collections, *Some Other Country* (2002) and *Icarus Sees His Father Fly* (2004), both with The Dedalus Press. His awards include the Seacat Irish National Poetry Prize, the Ireland Funds Prize, and the Hennessy/ Sunday Tribune Poetry Award. He lives in Dublin.

MARY O'DONNELL was born in Co. Monaghan. Her fifth poetry collection, *The Place of Miracles: New and Selected Poems* was published in 2006 by New Island Books. Her new short story collection will be published in 2008. She served on the jury of the International IMPAC Dublin Literary Award in 2006 and is a member of Aosdána.

DESMOND O'GRADY was born in Limerick in 1935. He is well-known both as a poet and translator. His latest collection is *On My Way* (Dedalus Press, 2006), and his translation *Ten Modern Arab Poets*, first published in 1992, was reissued in 2007. He is a member of Aosdána.

TOM O'MALLEY was born in Mayo in 1942. In 1984 he won the Patrick Kavanagh Poetry Award. His most recent collection By Lough Mask (Beaver Row Press, 1998) was awarded the 1998/9 Meath County Council/Tyrone Gutherie Centre Regional Bursary.

CAITRÍONA O'REILLY was born in Dublin in 1973 and lives Wicklow. She has published two collections of poetry: *The Nowhere Birds* (2001) and *The Sea Cabinet* (2006), both from Bloodaxe Books.

FRANK ORMSBY was born in 1947 in Enniskillen, Co. Fermanagh. His collections include *The Ghost Train* (The Gallery Press, 1995). He was Editor of *The Honest Ulsterman* and *Poetry Ireland Review*. His awards include the Cultural Traditions Award (1992) and the Lawrence O'Shaughnessy Award for Poetry (2002).

CATHAL Ó SEARCAIGH was born in Donegal in 1956. His selected poems, *Ag Tnúth leis an tSolas* (2001), won the Irish Times Irish-Language Prize. He has recently published *Seal in Neípeal* (2003), a memoir of a journey in Nepal. He is a member of Aosdána.

MICHEAL O'SIADHAIL has published twelve collections of poetry, including *Globe* (2007), *Love Life* (2005), *The Gossamer Wall: Poems in Witness to the Holocaust* (2002) and *Poems 1975-1995* (1995), all from Bloodaxe Books. Several have been published in Japan where he has given many readings and lectures. He is a member of Aosdána.

EOGHAN Ó TUAIRISC (Eugene Watters) was born in Co. Galway in 1919. In 1964 he published the long poem *The Week-end of Dermot and Grace* and the collection *Lux Aeterna*, which contains 'Aifreann na Marbh', his poetic Mass for the Hiroshima victims. He died in 1982.

JUSTIN QUINN was born in Dublin in 1968 and now lives in Prague. His latest book of poems is *Waves & Trees* (The Gallery Press, 2006).

PADRAIG ROONEY was born in Monaghan in 1956. His first collection, *In the Bonsai Garden*, won the Patrick Kavanagh Award in 1988. His second collection, *The Escape Artist*, was published in 2006 by Smith/Doorstop Books. He was Head of English at St. Maur International School in Yokohama from 1992-1996.

MARK ROPER is the author of four collections of poetry, most recently *Whereabouts* (Peterloo/Abbey Press, 2005). He was Editor of *Poetry Ireland Review* in 1999.

GABRIEL ROSENSTOCK was born in Co. Limerick in 1949. He is the author and translator of over a hundred books, including the bilingual *Rogha Dánta: Selected Poems* (Cló Iar-Chonnachta, 2005) and *The Year of the Goddess* (Dedalus Press, 2007). He is a member of Aosdána.

RICHARD RYAN was born in Dublin in 1946. He served as First Secretary at the Irish Embassy in Tokyo in the 1970s and was Ambassador to the Republic of Korea in the late 1980s and early 1990s. He has published two collections of poetry: *Ledges* (1970) and *Ravenswood* (1973), both with The Dolmen Press.

JOHN W. SEXTON was born in 1958. His most recent poetry collections are *Shadows Bloom / Scáthanna Faoi Bhláth*, a book of haiku with translations into Irish by Gabriel Rosenstock, and *Vortex* (Doghouse, 2005). He was awarded the Listowel Poetry Prize in 2007 for best single poem.

EILEEN SHEEHAN was born in 1963. Her work is widely published in journals and magazines. She is winner of the Brendan Kennelly Poetry Prize for 2006. Her collection *Song Of The Midnight Fox* is published by Doghouse Books, and her second collection is due in Spring 2008.

JAMES SIMMONS was born in Derry in 1933. His poetry collections include *The Company of Children* (Salmon Poetry, 1999) and *Mainstream* (Salmon Poetry, 1995). He died in 2001.

PETER SIRR was born in Waterford in 1960. A freelance writer, editor and translator, he is currently Editor of Poetry Ireland Review. He has published seven collections of poetry with The Gallery Press, most recently *Nonetheless* (2004) and *Selected Poems* (2004). He lives in Dublin.

GERARD SMYTH was born in 1951 in Dublin, where he still lives and works as a journalist. His poetry has been published widely in Ireland, Britain and the United States, as well as in translation. The most recent of his six collections are *A New Tenancy* (Dedalus Press, 2004) and *The Mirror Tent* (Dedalus Press, 2007).

BILL TINLEY was born in 1965. His first collection, *Grace*, appeared in 2001 from New Island Books. He received the Patrick Kavanagh Award in 1996. A selection of his poetry in Hungarian translation is due from Argumentum.

MACDARA WOODS was born in Dublin in 1942. He has published sixteen books, mostly poetry, as well as CDs and musical collaborations. He is the co-editor of the literary magazine *Cyphers*. A member of Aosdána, he lives in Dublin, and, when he can, in Umbria.

Further biographical and bibliographical information on many of the writers included in this volume can be found on Irish Writers Online (www.irishwriters-online.com), the website maintained by poet and novelist Philip Casey. Links to many of the publishers of these writers may be found on the Dedalus Press links page (www.dedaluspress.com/links.html).

ACKNOWLEDGEMENTS

Permission to use copyright material is gratefully acknowledged to the following:

Fergus Allen: 'Battue' from *Gas Light & Coke* (Dedalus Press, 2006). Dermot Bolger: 'First Japanese Sonnet', 'Second Japanese Sonnet' and 'Westport Tanka' from *Internal Exiles* (Dolmen Press, 1986). Pat Boran: 'A Natural History of Armed Conflict' from *As the Hand, the Glove* (Dedalus Press, 2001); 'Way of Peace' from *The Shape of Water* (Dedalus Press, 1996). David Burleigh: by permission of the author. Paddy Bushe: 'Frog Song' and 'Lótus Bhéarra' / 'Lotus in Beara' from *The Nitpicking of Cranes* (Dedalus Press, 2004). Ruth Carr: 'In Hokkaido' and 'Mushroom' from *There is a House* (Summer Palace Press, 1999). Ciaran Carson: Haikus from *Belfast Confetti* (The Gallery Press, 1989); 'The Rising Sun', 'Green Tea', 'The Irish Exile Michael Hinds', 'The Blue Shamrock', 'Fuji Film', 'Banana Tree' and 'February Fourteen' from *The Twelfth of Never* (The Gallery Press, 1999). Deirdre Cartmill: 'Karaoke in the Glasshouse' from *Midnight Solo* (Lagan Press, 2004). Juanita Casey: 'Zen and Now' from *Eternity Smith and Other Poems* (Dolmen Press, 1985). Austin Clarke: 'Japanese Print' from *Flight to Africa and Other Poems* (Dolmen Press, 1963), C/o R. Dardis Clarke, 17 Oscar Square, Dublin 8. Patrick Cotter: by permission of the author. Yvonne Cullen: 'Kabuki' from *Invitation to the Air* (Italics Press, 1998). Tony Curtis: 'Siren Off Inisheer', 'Northern Haiku' and 'Seven Haiku for Sahoko's Drawing' from *The Well in the Rain: New and Selected Poems* (Arc, 2006). Gerald Dawe: 'The Moon Viewing Room' by permission of the author. Patrick Deeley: 'Bashō on the Dodder' by permission of the author. Greg Delanty: 'The Speakeasy Oath' from *The Blind Stitch* (Carcanet Press, 2001). Moyra Donaldson: 'Kobi' from *Snakeskin Stilettos* (Lagan Press, 1998); 'Bamboo' and 'Carp' from *The Horse's Nest* (Lagan Press, 2006). Katie Donovan: 'Blossom Time' from *Entering the Mare* (Bloodaxe Books, 1997). Mary Dorcey: 'Grace' from *Like Joy In Season, Like Sorrow* (Salmon Press, 2001). Katherine Duffy: 'Nightingales of the Little Emperors' from *The Erratic Behaviour of Tides* (Dedalus Press, 1998). Seán Dunne: 'The Frail Sprig', 'The Art of Tea', 'A Shrine for Lafcadio Hearn, 1850-1904' and 'Shiatsu Sequence' from *Collected Poems* (The Gallery Press, 2005). Paul Durcan: 'Wild Sports of Japan', '6.30 a.m., 13 January 2004, Hokkaido Prefecture', 'Raftery in Tokyo', 'The Journey Home from Japan' and 'Facing Extinction' from *The Art of Life* (Harvill Press, 2004). Desmond Egan: 'Hiroshima' from *Paper Cranes Japanese and English* (Kandai Press, 1995). John Ennis: 'Watching the Descent of Yuichiro Miura' from *In a Green Shade* (Dedalus Press, 1991). Peter Fallon: 'World Peace' from *News of the World: Selected and New Poems* (The Gallery Press, 1998). Gerard Fanning: by permission of the author. Andrew Fitzsimons: 'Worlds', 'Ornaments' and 'The Human' from *Emerging from Absence: An Archive of Japan in English-Language Verse* (2003); 'The Risen Tide' from *Fortnight* ; 'The Autumn Night' and 'A Letter' from *The Dublin Review*; 'Shunkashūto' from *Poetry Ireland Review*. Anthony Glavin: extracts from 'Living in Hiroshima' from *The Wrong Side of the Alps* (The Gallery Press, 1989). Mark Granier: 'The Great Wave– Hokusai' from *Airborne* (Salmon Poetry, 2001). Pamela Greene: 'Waiting for You' from *Tattoo Me* (Summer Palace Press, 2002). Eamon Grennan: 'Sunshine, Salvation,

Drying Shirt' from *Relations* (Graywolf, 1999). Maurice Harmon: 'Japanese Garden' and 'Afternoon Tea' from *The Last Regatta* (Salmon Poetry, 2000). Michael Hartnett: extracts from 'Inchicore Haiku' from *Collected Poems* (The Gallery Press, 2001). Francis Harvey: 'A Tanka and Four Haiku' from *Collected Poems* (Dedalus Press, 2007). Seamus Heaney: '1.1.87' from *Seeing Things* (Faber & Faber, 1991); 'The Strand' from *The Spirit Level* (Faber & Faber, 1997); 'Fiddleheads' and 'Midnight Anvil' from *District and Circle* (Faber & Faber, 2006); 'Petals on a Bough' by permission of the author. Rachael Hegarty: by permission of the author. John Hewitt: 'Gloss, on the Difficulties of Translation' from *The Selected Poems of John Hewitt*, ed. Michael Longley & Frank Ormsby (Blackstaff Press, 2007), reproduced by permission of Blackstaff Press on behalf of the Estate of John Hewitt. John Hughes: 'Nagasaki' from *Negotiations with the Chill Wind* (The Gallery Press, 1991). Pearse Hutchinson: 'Sneachta i gCuach Airgid' / 'Snow in a Silver Bowl' from *The Soul that Kissed the Body* (The Gallery Press, 1990); 'Koan' from *Barnsley Main Seam* (The Gallery Press, 2002). Biddy Jenkinson: 'Tóraíocht Tai Haku sna plandlannaí' from *Amhras Neimhe* (Coiscéim, 1997). Fred Johnston: 'The Blue Whale' from *Paris Without Maps* (Northwords Press, 2002). Eileen Kato: 'Sakurajima' from *Journal of Irish Studies*. Neville Keery: 'Far Away' from *Turnings* (Hinds Publishing, 1999). Thomas Kinsella: 'Old Harry' from *Collected Poems* (Carcanet Press, 2001). Matt Kirkham: 'Unfinished Haiku' from *Poetry Introductions 1* (Lagan Press, 2004). Anatoly Kudryavitsky: 'Unobana in Full Bloom' from *Morning at Mount Ring* (Doghouse, 2007). Michael Longley: 'A Gift of Boxes', 'A Grain of Rice', 'A Pair of Shoes', 'The Weather in Japan', 'Birds & Flowers' and 'White Water' from *Collected Poems* by Michael Longley (Jonathan Cape, 2006). Brian Lynch: 'The Tea Ceremony' from *New and Renewed: Poems 1967-2004* (New Island, 2004). Derek Mahon: 'The Snow Party' from *Collected Poems* (The Gallery Press, 1999); 'Bashō in Kinsale' from *Harbour Lights* (The Gallery Press, 2005). Aidan Carl Mathews: 'Bashō's Rejected Jottings' from *Minding Ruth* (The Gallery Press, 1983). John McAuliffe: 'Japan' from *Next Door* (The Gallery Press, 2007). James McCabe: from 'Cliara Haiku I—XXX' from *The White Battlefield of Silence* (Dedalus Press, 1999). Thomas McCarthy: 'Japanese Bell' from *The Non-Aligned Storyteller* (Anvil Press, 1984). Medbh McGuckian: 'The Flower Master' from *The Flower Master* (The Gallery Press, 1982) and 'The Butterfly Farm' and 'The Bird Calendar' (c/o The Gallery Press). Peter McMillan: 'Broken Ink Landscape' by permission of the author; Translation of the Ogura Hyakunin Isshu from *One Hundred Poems One Poem Each* (Columbia University Press, 2007). Ted McNulty: 'Dreaming in Japanese' from *The Irish Times*; C/o Sheila O'Hagan. Paula Meehan: by permission of the author. Dorothy Molloy: 'Four Haikus' from *Gethsemane Day* (Faber & Faber, 2006). Sinéad Morrissey: 'Goldfish', 'Night Drive in Four Metaphors', 'Between Here and There', 'Nagasawa in Training' and 'To Encourage the Study of Kanji' from *Between Here and There* (Carcanet Press, 2002). Paul Muldoon: 'The Narrow Road to the Deep North' from *Mules* (Faber & Faber, 1977); 'Sushi' from *Meeting the British* (Faber & Faber, 1987); 'The Point', 'Nighingales', and extracts from 'Hopewell Haiku' from *Hay* (Faber& Faber, 1998). Gerry Murphy: 'The Ferbane Haiku' and 'Haiku for Norman McCaig' and 'Ballynoe Haiku' from *End of Part One: New & Selected Poems* (Dedalus Press, 2006). Nuala Ní Dhomhnaill: 'Sneachta'/'Snow' from *Selected Poems* (New Island,

2000). Julie O' Callaghan: 'Time', 'Lady Hyobu', 'A View of Mount Fuji' and 'Two Lines' from *Tell Me This Is Normal: New and Selected Poems* (Bloodaxe Books, 2008); '21st Century Pillow Book' and 'Calligraphy' by permission of the author. John O'Donnell: 'The Wave' from *Poetry Ireland Review*. Mary O'Donnell: '10 Haikus on Love and Death' from *The Place of Miracles: New and Selected Poems* (New Island, 2006). Desmond O'Grady: extracts from 'Summer Harvest Renga' from *On My Way* (Dedalus Press, 2006). Tom O' Malley: extracts from 'Seasonal Haiku' from *Journey Backward* (Salmon Poetry, 1998). Caitríona O'Reilly: 'Netsuke' from *The Sea Cabinet* (Bloodaxe Books, 2006). Frank Ormsby: by permission of the author. Cathal Ó Searcaigh: 'Duine Corr' / 'Odd Man Out' and 'Pilleadh an Deoraí' / 'Exile's Return' from *By the Hearth in Mín a' Leá* (Arc 2005). Micheal O'Siadhail: 'Tsunami' from *Globe* (Bloodaxe Books, 2007). Eoghan Ó Tuairisc: c/o Rita Kelly, extracts from 'Aifreann na Marbh' from *Lux Aeterna* (Cois Life, 2000), and English translations from *Poetry Ireland Review*. Justin Quinn: 'On Speed' from *The 'O'o'a'a' Bird* (Carcanet Press, 1995). Padraig Rooney: 'In the Bonsai Garden' from *In the Bonsai Garden* (Raven Arts Press, 1988); 'Sukiaki' and 'The Night Golfer' by permission of the author. Mark Roper: from *Whereabouts* (Abbey Press, 2005). Gabriel Rosenstock: 'A Handful of Haiku in Irish and English' from *The SHOp;* 'Farrera' (*Emerging from Absence: An Archive of Japan in English-Langauge Verse,* 2007). Richard Ryan: by permission of the author. John W. Sexton: 'Issa in the golden corridor' from *Shadows Bloom / Scáthanna Faoi Bláth* (Doghouse, 2004). Eileen Sheehan: 'claiming it' from *Versal.* James Simmons: 'Empire' from *The Company of Children* (Salmon Poetry, 1999). Peter Sirr: 'In the Japanese Garden' from *Marginal Zones* (The Gallery Press, 1984). Gerard Smyth: 'December Moon' by permission of the author. Bill Tinley: 'Jeanne Hébuterne' from *Grace* (New Island, 2001). Joseph Woods: 'Sailing to Hokkaido', 'Where the Word for Beautiful is Clean', 'New Year's Day, Nagasaki', 'Triptych' and 'Persimmon' from *Sailing to Hokkaido* (Worple Press, 2001). Macdara Woods: 'Rosbeg, July 2nd, 1970' from *Knowledge in the Blood: New and Selected Poems* (The Dedalus Press, 2000).

Every effort has been made to contact copyright holders. The publishers would be grateful to have any omissions brought to their attention.

Poetry from Ireland and the world

Established in 1985, the Dedalus Press is one of Ireland's longest established and best known literary imprints, dedicated to new Irish poetry and to poetry from around the world in English translation. Last year's publication of *On Two Shores: New and Selected Poems* by Mutsuo Takahashi (translated by Mitsuko Ohno and Frank Sewell), and published in a bilingual Japanese-English edition, was the first by a Japanese poet on our international list, so we are especially pleased to be involved now with the publication of *Our Shared Japan*, a book which represents some small part of an ongoing and, it would appear, mutually inspiring international dialogue.

For its support in the production of this volume, we express our grateful thanks to the Cultural Division of the Department of Foreign Affairs and to Poetry Ireland.

For further information on this and other Dedalus Press publications, see
www.dedaluspress.com